LOCKHEED
L1011
TriStar

C000269084

LOCKHEED
L1011
TriStar

Philip Birtles

MBI Publishing Company

This edition first published in 1998 by MBI Publishing Company,
729 Prospect Avenue, PO Box 1, Osceola, WI 54020-0001 USA.

© 1998 Philip Birtles

Previously published by Airlife Publishing Ltd, Shrewsbury, England.

All rights reserved. With the exception of quoting brief passages
for the purposes of review no part of this publication may be
reproduced without prior written permission from the Publisher.

The information in this book is true and complete to the best of
our knowledge. All recommendations are made without any
guarantee on the part of the author or publisher, who also disclaim
any liability incurred in connection with the use of this data or
specific details.

We recognize that some words, model names and designations,
for example, mentioned herein are the property of the trademark
holder. We use them for identification purposes only. This is not
an official publication.

MBI Publishing Company books are also available at discounts in
bulk quantity for industrial or sales-promotional use. For details
write to Special Sales Manager at Motorbooks International Wholesalers &
Distributors, 729 Prospect Avenue, PO Box 1, Osceola, WI 54020-0001 USA.

Library of Congress Cataloging-in-Publication Data available

ISBN 0-7603-0582-X

Printed in Singapore

CONTENTS

INTRODUCTION

The TriStar, Lockheed's only commercial jet airliner, was launched at a time of rampant inflation and the financial penalties almost brought the company to ruin. Not only were the launch costs too great for one organisation, but the TriStar was not successful enough to allow the company to reap the dividends of its development costs by launching a family of jet airliners, bringing a broader customer base. Instead, Lockheed was left with all the eggs all in one basket: and unprofitable eggs they were too.

On the positive side, the Lockheed L1011 TriStar brought new standards of technology and safety to wide-bodied fan-jet powered airliners. It has proved long-lived — it may now be approaching the twilight of its career, but there are still substantial numbers of the original fleet in service 25 years after the type was first introduced, a fair proportion still in operation with the original airlines. Delta still has many of its original aircraft and acquired further examples as they were put up for disposal by other operators. TriStars are also still flying with Saudia, BWIA, Royal Jordanian, TAP and AirLanka where they continue to give good service, despite the inevitable increase of maintenance costs associated with all aging airliners. With the aircraft purchase costs long paid for, the Rolls-Royce RB211 engines still giving good service and the equipment fit proving the excellence of the original design — which included autoland capability — the TriStars are still commercially viable today. In addition, although some TriStars are stored in the desert, few have been scrapped because they have reached the end of their structural life — and the active conversion programme into freighters is likely to absorb some of the surplus airframes over the next few years, keeping the TriStar in the skies for the foreseeable future.

Writing a book of this nature can often be a lonely exercise

while seeking out the research material, but it is the unselfish help of others which helps to bring life into such an undertaking. Thanks are therefore due to Flt Lt David Rowe, the Community Relations Officer of RAF Brize Norton; the crew of TriStar ZD953, Flt Lt Ken McRedie, Flt Lt Paul Rogers, S/L George Roberts, Flt Lt Peter Goodman and Sgt Chris Carrol; the crew of VC-10 XR807 led by Flt Lt Neil Purves; Linda Lloyd and staff at Marshall Aerospace; Raul Alves Fernandes of TAP Air Portugal, Miss Deepthi Edirisinghe of AirLanka, Mario Mattarelli of Royal, Niclas Baath and Kjell Westfalt of Blue Scandinavia, Kevin H. Coffman of Lockheed Martin, Johann Prozesky with Gulf Air and Stewart Wilson of SW Media in Australia. Without their help this book would certainly lack in pictures and updated information. The book would not have been written at all without the unselfish support and advice of my wife Martha.

BELOW: The new British Airways TriStar 500 G-BFCA, the first L1011-500 built, was displayed at the Farnborough Air Show in September 1980. It is seen here just after touch down with the reverse thrust deployed on the RB211 engines. *Philip Birtles*

1 EVOLUTION

COMPETITION

The Lockheed Corporation was one of the big three commercial airline producers on the West Coast of the United States at the end of World War II, the others being Boeing and Douglas. While Britain had concentrated on the urgent need for combat aircraft during hostilities — fighters and bombers — American industry not only supported this country with additional combat aircraft, but also had the capacity to undertake the design, development and production of transport aircraft. These were to play a major role in winning World War II for the Allies, while at the same time giving the US aerospace industry a head start when peace came — and not just in the internal US marketplace, but internationally too

The prewar market leader was undoubtedly Douglas, which had a well-established reputation before World War II and the most successful prewar aircraft — the brilliant two-engined DC-3, over 10,000 of every type of which would be built. The four-engined DC-4 design gave Douglas a basic aircraft suitable for postwar development and would lead to the longer and more powerful DC-6 and ultimately the DC-7; on top of this, the sheer quantity of DC-3s and DC-4s produced as a military transports meant that many airlines in the immediate postwar years would use second-hand Douglas aircraft. This is best exemplified by the DC-4, whose production run was taken over by the USAAF after Pearl Harbor: over 1,000

were produced — mainly as C-54 Skymasters for the military — but fewer than 100 of these were built for civilian operators.

Boeing, meanwhile, today's massive market leader, had made its reputation during the war by producing bombers — the B-17 Flying Fortress and B-29 Superfortress — which would be adapted postwar for civil use. The long-range B-29/B-50 series (the B-50 was the improved postwar version) became the double-decked Stratocruiser, the clipper of the skies, replacing the flying boats. Its successor was the United States' first commercial jet airliner, the aircraft which firmly established Boeing's rise to success in the jet era, the Boeing 707. It was the first of a series of Boeing medium and long-range aircraft which would dominate the airline markets of the last quarter of the 20th century.

LOCKHEED

The Lockheed Corporation — successor to the Loughead brothers' various concerns — had produced a number of important civil aircraft before the war under the design aegis of well-known designers such as Jack Northrop, Jerry Vultee, Lloyd Stearman and, of course, Clarence 'Kelly' Johnson, who would be responsible for so many ground-breaking engineering designs. The prewar Vega, Orion and Electra/Junior Electra/Super Electra family were credible alternatives to the Douglas DC-2 and DC-3. By the end of the war Lockheed had produced nearly seven percent of the US aircraft built during hostilities, which ranked the company fifth largest in the United States. It had built mainly the P-38 Lightning, A-28/-29 Hudson, C-56 Lodestar, P-80 Shooting Star, PV-1 Ventura, PV-2 Harpoon, B-17 Flying Fortresses under licence — and the graceful Constellation. Conceived in the

BELOW: Lockheed played a significant part in the commercial airliner business with its Constellation, developed before World War II, and adapted for military use during the hostilities. Following the end of the war, the Constellation re-entered the commercial field, while also giving continuing good service with the US services. USAF C-121C 40153, used by the Military Air Transport Service, is now preserved at Charleston AFB in South Carolina. *Lockheed*

TOP: The ultimate piston-engined airliner was the Lockheed Starliner, the final commercial development of the Constellation. 44 were built, mainly for TWA, Air France and Lufthansa. *Lockheed*

ABOVE: Lockheed's first postwar airliner was the prop-jet Electra. *Philip Birtles*

te 1930s, the Constellation was an outstanding piston-engined esign, which combined high speed with reliable and economic perations giving it excellent passenger appeal. However, the art of hostilities precluded commercial operations and the Constellation was ordered for the USAAF.

Lockheed's military sales continued postwar in the 1950s nd 1960s with the jet-powered P-80, the Neptune, the T-33 ainer, the Mach 2 F-104 Starfighter, the ubiquitous C-130 Hercules, the P-3 Orion, the C-141 Starlifter and the enormous -5 Galaxy. On top of this, Kelly Johnson's Burbank 'Skunk orks' would produce the highly secret U-2 and TR-1 spy-lanes and would go on to produce the acme of 'strategic recon-aissance' aircraft — the SR-71. With this background and an nnovative design team, it could have been expected that ockheed would compete strongly in the postwar civil airliner narket. This was not the case; untypically the company choose conservative route, producing the prop-jet Electra, which, lthough economic to operate, did not have the passenger ppeal of the jets and failed to find a significant market. (It did, owever, gain world-wide success when it was adapted as the -3 Orion maritime patrol aircraft.) Lockheed, therefore, lost ut on the first stage of the jet airliner development.

In the early 1960s Lockheed looked at two commercial pro-cts at Burbank. The first, in 1963, was the stillborn American SST. Lockheed proposed a fixed-wing slim-delta layout similar to a scaled up Concorde; the competing Boeing design featured a variable geometry swing-wing. The Boeing project gained official approval, but it was then found that the swing-wing design would not meet the airline payload/range requirements, and therefore a change was made to the slim-delta layout before the programme was abandoned altogether as being totally uneconomic. Meanwhile the Lockheed Georgia Company was developing the large C-5 tactical transport for the USAF, and there were studies at Palmdale for turning that aircraft into a commercial airliner; these were later abandoned. It was in fact the Electra programme which eventually led to the TriStar.

During the preliminary design studies for the maritime patrol aircraft which eventually led to the P-3C Orion, two, three and four-jet engined layouts were considered. They fea-tured the long narrow fuselage and big fuel-filled wings that would give the long endurance required by the US Navy. One of the twin-engined designs looked quite promising, but was rejected by the USN as being too risky for long over-water

flights in case of engine failure. (This was before the era of ETOPS — extended-range twin-engined operations — which has seen two-engined airliners permitted to extend their over-water flying times because engine technology has reached the position of being able to guarantee a high level of reliability.) Despite this rejection, the project still appeared to have some advantages, and the P-3C team continued to study the concept in its spare time. The resulting layout was a flat-oval shaped wide-bodied fuselage with accommodation for 250 passengers in a twin aisle layout. It had a high wing with a pair of large fan engines mounted in underwing pods. Although performance was briefly checked on a wind tunnel model, pressure of work for the US government on the Orion resulted in these airliner schemes being put to one side.

In the latter part of 1966, just a few months before the Lockheed SST proposals were rejected, American Airlines published an outline specification for a large capacity, short to medium range airliner powered by the planned new technology large turbofan engines then being developed. Despite the direct competition from the Douglas DC-10, Lockheed decided to use this requirement as the basis for its re-entry into the commercial jet airliner market. Unfortunately for Lockheed,

American Airlines became the launch customer for the DC-10 when the company placed its order to Douglas on 19 February 1968. This made it all the more important that Lockheed seek a launch contract in order to be a part of the prospective new business in wide-bodied jet airliners. Boeing did not, at that time, threaten direct competition; the company was fully concerned with the longer range, high capacity 747.

Although rejected by American Airlines, Lockheed had worked closely with the airline to define the specification of its aircraft. The requirement was for a 300-passenger airliner with a similar performance to the lower-capacity second-generation jet airliners, but with better economics and quieter engines. This meant a Mach 0.8 cruise and operations from a 9,000ft (2,700m) runway on a hot day. Although American was happy with a one-stop, USA transcontinental range of 2,130 miles (3,400km), other potential operators regarded non-stop US transcontinental range as essential.

The American Airlines' specification was probably too restrictive for the overall market needs, and it is very easy for a manufacturer to fall into the trap of trying to satisfy a very specialised need to achieve an order. American Airlines was faced with restrictions because of its investment in La Guardia

a big twin-engined aircraft similar in concept to the earlier, shelved, adaptation of the US Navy maritime patrol aircraft design. These schemes were pulled out and dusted down as a basis for a new high density, medium-range airliner.

During the latter half of 1966, a more detailed exploration was made of the wide-bodied twin by a primary design group. The group looked at an aircraft whose size was between the first-generation narrow-bodied Boeing 707 and the larger Boeing 747. With the loss of the SST programme in December 1966, Lockheed had surplus engineering capacity of about 1,200 staff, many of whom were transferred to the new airliner project, giving it a high level of priority. Continuing contacts with the major US domestic trunk operators at the time helped define the overall objectives and requirements. Although the payload was to be doubled on the short to medium-haul routes, passenger comfort and appeal had to be improved. There needed to be an increase in economy and cruising speed without affecting the existing airport facilities. Higher utilisation was required through faster turn-round, and reliability needed to be improved, allied to design for easier maintenance. Reduced operating costs, quieter engine operation and automatic landing capability were required, again, to improve reliability. In this latter capability, the TriStar scored strongly over the competition for many years, as, on the North Atlantic run from the USA to Europe during the winter months, a morning arrival with fog is not uncommon. While the TriStar could almost certainly guarantee arrival at the planned destination, other less-sophisticated long-haul aircraft may have been faced with an unwelcome diversion.

All this new technology and improved economical performance was required to provide a good return on the initial capital investment for the aircraft, — an aircraft which, it was hoped, would be the start of what was to become a family of models extending the scope of operations, while retaining commonality in spares, maintenance, support, ground handling and training.

Airport in New York. The terminal area had geometric and dimensional restraints, and the piers used to support the runway extension over the bay caused a weight restriction of 270,000lb (122,580kg), although these piers have since been strengthened. The ultimate aim of the brief American specification was to carry the maximum number of passengers at a minimum cost per seat mile, which, without the La Guardia restrictions, meant

ABOVE LEFT: The concept which eventually led to the TriStar also sired the Lockheed P-3C Orion maritime patrol aircraft. Produced at Marietta, Georgia, this US Navy Orion is flying over the significant local landmark of Stone Mountain. *Lockheed*

BELOW: The TriStar's major competitor was the look-alike McDonnell Douglas DC-10. *McDonald Douglas via Günter Endres*

2 DESIGN

ABOVE: By mid-1967 Lockheed had begun to favour the tri-jet configration for its new L1011 family of wide-bodied airliners, the configuration being tested in the wind tunnel. *Lockheed*

PLANS AND PARAMETERS

During the studies to meet the new design's demanding requirements, the Lockheed design team evaluated 66 different configurations leading to a basic layout in the early months of 1967. The layout was a circular-section wide-bodied fuselage with a pair of the new fan engines mounted under either a low or mid-wing, the designation being CL1011-28. It was planned to carry 250 passengers up to 1,600 miles (2,500km) with a gross weight of 300,000lb (136,000kg). Overall dimensions were a wingspan of 155ft (47m) and a length of 162ft (50m). Although the economics of the twin appeared more promising, studies of three-engined layouts were also made under the designations CL1011-30, -31, -32 and -33.

Lockheed was prudent to look further than just the American Airlines' requirement, to establish a broader basis for the overall design needs. Eastern, for example, preferred a trijet, as its longest non-stop route was 1,800 miles (2,900km), much of it over water — and in the era before ETOPS a twin would not have been suitable for this. Meanwhile TWA, which was just starting to introduce the new Boeing 747, was also interested in a smaller wide-bodied aircraft for its domestic routes — routes where the 747 was too large and uneconomic, particularly on Chicago–Los Angeles, as well as Kansas and St Louis to West Coast destinations. With the natural barrier of the Rockies on these routes, TWA preferred a tri-jet, as a single engine diversion would require each engine to be able to develop 55,000lb (245kN) of thrust, and no such engine existed at that time. Both airlines favoured the wide-bodied high-density fuselage with seating for between 250 and 300 passengers.

As the discussions with the potential operators continued during 1967, it became clear that US transcontinental range was essential, and by September the airlines were being offered the L1011-365 with a capacity of 227 passengers and a gross weight of 320,000lb (145,000kg). The third engine had been added in the rear fuselage with the air intake on top of the fuselage at the base of the fin leading edge. It was anticipated that the power of each of the three engines would be around 35,000lb (156kN) thrust. With a high level of automatic flight operations combined with the three engines, there would be fewer restrictions on take-off and landing in poor visibility and improved performance and safety in the event of an engine failure. It would also be possible to make two-engined ferry flights to allow corrective maintenance at a main engineering base rather than having to set up expensive maintenance away from the correct facilities. The three-engine layout gave a better basis for development as the engine power increased in the normal way, and the final decision was made for three engines, when it was realised that over the critical shorter ranges the tri-jet was no more expensive than the twin.

At the beginning of 1968 both Lockheed and McDonnell Douglas were refining their designs ready for the anticipated large orders from the US airlines. Lockheed had refined its L1011-385 to a longer fuselage of 175ft (53m) with room for up to 250 passengers, and a capability of operating economically from the 7,000ft (2,100m) runway at New York's La Guardia to Chicago. By then the engines were expected to develop 37,000lb (165kN) thrust and, although ideal for the American Airlines operations, the range did not suit the coast-to-coast requirements of TWA and Eastern. With the choice of the DC-10 by American, Lockheed was able to concentrate on the transcontinental range capability for other carriers. At this stage the new airliner was named TriStar, in accordance with the company's tradition of naming its aircraft after heavenly bodies.

To cope with the demands of the potential operators, the TriStar had grown to an all-up-weight of 409,000lb (186,000kg) by March 1968, giving a payload capability of 56,200lb (25,500kg), equivalent to a maximum of 345 passengers. By then the engine thrust had grown to 40,000lb (178kN) giving a cruising speed of Mach 0.8 at 35,000ft (10,700m) over typical ranges of 3,300 miles (5,300km). This made the TriStar much more competitive at exactly the right time because, although the DC-10 had won the first order, the order had not been sufficient to launch that programme; the sales battle between Lockheed and McDonnell Douglas intensified! In an effort to influence the decision-making process of both Eastern and TWA, Lockheed offered very favourable terms in the buyers' market, a policy which was to have a far-reaching effect, as events were subsequently to show.

Both the airlines were well aware of the effect of their choice on the manufacturers, and quite naturally took full advantage of their bargaining position. Working together, both airlines decided in principle at board meetings on 26 March 1968 to order the TriStar, but kept the decision secret while they held further discussions with both Lockheed and McDonnell Douglas the next day at the Waldorf Astoria Hotel in New York. A press conference had been scheduled at the hotel for 11.00am on 29 March to announce the selection of the aircraft, but it was not until only the evening of the 28th that TWA came to an agreement with Lockheed and advised Eastern and McDonnell Douglas of its decision. Eastern confirmed its selection of the TriStar later the same evening, and the letters of intent were signed over breakfast, ready for the scheduled press conference launching the TriStar into development. The orders, worth $2,160 million (£1,080 million), were a record for an airliner still on the drawing board.

As defined the initial version of the TriStar would seat up to 270 passengers in a mixed-class layout, or up to 300 all-economy seats. In the mixed-class layout, the aircraft had the full transcontinental capability; in all-economy it could operate from La Guardia to Chicago even on a hot day. Power was from three new Rolls-Royce RB211 large fan engines giving high power with low fuel consumption and quiet operation. The TriStar had a growth capability to match the anticipated increase thrust of the engines to 50,000lb (222kN). With provision for additional fuel tankage in the wing centre-section and fin, the TriStar would be capable of transatlantic range. Thoughts were also being given to an ultra-high density short-range version with a fuselage stretch of 40ft (12m) to give an all-economy class load of 400 passengers. With the European Airbus programme getting under way, some consideration was being given again to the reduced-fuselage length twin-engined versions for the short ranges.

The initial production version of the TriStar was set with a range of 3,160 miles (5,100km) carrying a payload of 56,200lb (25,515kg) at an economical cruising speed of 565mph (910kph), or Mach 0.85, at between 31,000 and 35,000ft (9,500–10,700m). At a gross weight of 409,000lb (186,000kg) it would take-off and clear an altitude of 35ft (10.5m) in a distance of 8,750ft (2,670m) at sea level in standard ISA conditions.

PROTOTYPE PRODUCTION

Manufacture of the first TriStar commenced on 1 March 1969, actual assembly starting on 24 June. The first aircraft was built as the new factory was constructed around it. The first fuselage was completed in April 1970, with the cockpit and forward fuse-

lage being mated with the centre section in a massive docking jig. The rear cabin up to the rear pressure dome was then added, followed by the wings. In June, the RB211 engines were delivered and installed in the aircraft, the tail end was attached and the remainder of the equipment installed. Structurally complete on 20 July 1970, the official roll-out took place on 1 September.

In parallel with the production for flight development and customer deliveries, a fatigue test specimen airframe was built by December 1970, ready to start a demanding two-year programme to simulate 36,000 flights, to identify any possible faults well ahead of the flight test programme and operational flying. A static test specimen was also built and both test airframes were located in a special building as part of the overall systems and structural test programmes.

Following the official roll-out at Palmdale, the first TriStar was moved to the adjacent flight test hangar for the functional testing, installation of special instrumentation, engine runs and taxi tests in preparation for the first flight. On 16 November 1970, less than 21 months since assembly had commenced and two and a half years from the initial orders from Eastern and TWA, the first TriStar lifted-off from Palmdale on its maiden flight: in command was Project Pilot Hank Dees. Take-off weight was 330,000lb (151,000kg) including 85,000lb (38,600kg) of fuel and a payload of 40,000lb (18,000kg) of test equipment. Lift-off was at 152kts (282kph) after a run of 5,300ft (1,600m) and during the 2hr 30min flight a speed of 250kts (463kph) was achieved, and an altitude of 20,000ft (6,100m) was reached. Handling was better than predicted on the ground-based engineering simulator and the engines operated well. So started a demanding flight development programme involving six aircraft flying 1,700 hours in some 1,500 flights.

BELOW: TWA and Eastern worked closely together to place the launch orders for the TriStar, making their decisions in principle on 26 March 1968. TWA announced its confirmation to order TriStars on the evening of 28 March, ready for the press conference at the Waldorf Astoria Hotel in New York at 11.00hrs the next day. TWA TriStar 100 N31030 operated transatlantic services to London Heathrow and flew its last service with TWA on 30 October 1994 before being returned to its owners and put into desert storage. *Lockheed*

ABOVE: Full-scale fatigue and static test specimens were built for the TriStar, and located in a special building at Palmdale. *Lockheed*

FLIGHT TESTING

The maiden flight of the first TriStar, N1011, on 16 November 1970 was the start of an intensive 12-month 1,695-hour flight development programme involving the first five aircraft. The first flight was exactly to the schedule set two and a half years previously. Both the aircraft and engines performed well and the target for certification was 15 November 1971.

The flight development and test programme for the RB211 engines had already been underway for over eight months when the initial flight-cleared engine became airborne for the first time in a modified VC-10 from Hucknall on 6 March. The Rolls-Royce engine had been chosen by Lockheed on 29 March 1968 in the largest single export order ever achieved by British industry. The engine contract covered the complete power module, the airframe parts being subcontracted to Shorts Bros of Belfast. Detailed design of the engine had started in July 1967, the high bypass ratio of 5:1 resulting in the large front fan producing over 70 percent of the engine thrust giving quieter operation and greater economy. The engine was designed around seven independent modules, allowing easy and rapid change of any single module with the engine remaining on the aircraft. This determined the individual service life of each module, instead of taking the worst case for the whole engine. The original engine was expected to have a thrust approaching 40,000lb (178kN), later growing to 50,000lb (222kN) without any increase in diameter. The engine was also configured for the TriStar, allowing easy access for maintenance. A major advance for the engine was to have it configured with three concentric spools, rather than two, bringing greater efficiency in its compact size, and fewer moving parts to improve maintenance.

The first of the development engines ran initially on the ground test stand on 31 August 1968, and the development progressed as more engines became available to include climatic testing at the National Gas Turbine Establishment at Pyestock near Farnborough, where most of the TriStar flight envelope

BELOW: Shortly before the maiden flight, the TriStar prototype N1011 was taken out for taxy trials to check, amongst other things, the operation of the brakes. *Lockheed*

ABOVE: In command of the TriStar's maiden flight on 16 November 1970 was Hank Dees in the left-hand seat, with Ralph Cokely in the right-hand pilot's seat. Rod Bray (left) was the flight development team leader and the flight engineer was Glenn Fisher. *Lockheed*

could be simulated. Clearing the RB211 for flight commenced at the beginning of 1970, the test engine being installed in the much-modified port engine position of a VC-10 supplied by the RAF, replacing the pair of Conway engines. The engine was mounted as close as possible to the same installation as on the TriStar, using much of the associated equipment. The engine's flight development programme required 1,100 flying hours. The flight tests were able to explore the full flying performance of the TriStar, check all the operational requirements and establish engine management techniques, with the required flight-deck instrumentation. It was also possible to study accessibility, maintenance and spares requirements, while helping to establish initial service life. By the time of the first flight of the engine, 18 out of the 19 test bed engines were running, most to TriStar installation standards, and the prototype engines for the first aircraft were in production. The target thrust of 40,600lb (180kN) was achieved by the end of 1969, with fuel consumption to be confirmed by flight testing.

When the TriStar was being prepared for its maiden flight, six engines had already been delivered to Palmdale. The production standard engines were to follow for the second aircraft, with the target thrust being 42,000lb (187kN). Overall test running had reached 3,000 hours with the production engines

being used to establish endurance with fuel consumption on target. The three-shaft layout gave good engine response and low vibration levels, and on-condition maintenance would be possible from service entry. Although the early TriStar flight-test engines were cleared initially for only 50 hours' operation, they were progressively cleared on-condition for more hours as the test flying progressed.

Two days after its maiden flight, the first TriStar was airborne again to check low speed handling and the full functioning of the undercarriage and flaps. On this flight, a speed of 300kts (556kph) and an altitude of 10,000ft (3,000m) was reached. By early December, five flights had been made with shut-down tests of both the No 1 and No 2 engines, followed by successful relights. Total flying time in less than a month was nearly 25 hours, reaching a maximum speed of 350kts (648kph), and the take-off weight had reached 335,000lb (152,000kg). Air starts had been made on all three engines, with and without the assistance of the auxiliary power unit.

LEFT: Due to structural problems with lightweight composite blades, Rolls-Royce had to substitute titanium blades. Production continued of the early development RB211 engines at Derby, while the negotiations continued to finance the engine and aircraft programme. *Rolls-Royce*

In final assembly were 12 aircraft including the two structural test specimens, with the production rate building up to one aircraft a week one year after the maiden flight. While the flight development programme progressed, the structural test specimens were testing the integrity of the airframe well ahead of any flying, the fatigue specimen starting a two-year simulated programme of 36,000 flights in January 1971.

At the time of the financial failure of Rolls-Royce in February 1971, the prototype TriStar had flown about 40 hours, and the first two production aircraft were waiting to join the development programme. During this early testing, the prototype had achieved all its design targets, including flying at Mach 0.7 and 300kts (556kph) up to the cruise altitude of 30,000ft (9,150m). The fully forward and aft limits of the centre of gravity had been explored — the approach to the stall was ice free — and accelerated flight had been made with loads of up to 2g. Systems' testing had included air-starting the auxiliary power unit at 20,000ft (6,100m), and keeping it running up to 30,000ft (9,150m). In the event of a loss of engine power it was expected that a windmilling RB211 would provide enough emergency hydraulic power at above 200kts (370kph), but that at approach speeds of below 150kts (278kph), an emergency drop-out Dowty ram-air turbine would supplement the engine-driven systems, providing enough power for the flying controls and a safe landing.

The engines had behaved well, although fuel consumption was a little high, and they were tolerant to deliberate mishandling, including holding them in reverse thrust right down to zero forward speed at idle power. To minimise brake wear during taxying, the centre engine was run in reverse, and the engines were shut down and started in the reverse thrust configuration. Development engines had been arriving at Palmdale in time, but the production units were 6–12 months behind schedule.

The second TriStar, painted in TWA markings, made its maiden flight of 1hr 25min duration on 15 February 1971, testing the undercarriage, flaps, slats and spoilers, as well as the environmental control system, bringing total test flying to nearly 55 hours. During the financial negotiations to rescue the whole TriStar programme, flight testing did continue, but at a reduced rate. During this time the prototype was grounded for a month to allow time to catch up on modifications and to uprate the three pre-production engines. Upon return to the test programme, the prototype took-off from the long runway at Edwards AFB, lifting its heaviest load yet, 404,570lb (183,675kg). During this flight a top speed of 495kts (917kph) was reached at 30,000ft (9,150m), and the aircraft was airborne for 6hr 41min, more than twice its previous longest flight.

On 27 April the second TriStar made its first two automatic landings, following a touchdown with automatic control of the flying surfaces, but manual operation of the throttles. On certification, the TriStar was expected to be able to achieve Cat 2 standards of automatic flight control, with later development to Cat 3 capability. It was expected to comply with the new FAR36 noise regulations because of its high-volume low-velocity jet stream, assisted by noise-attenuated intake liners. The engines had continued to stand up well to rough handling, starting with a 20kt (37kph) tailwind and taxying with a 50kt (93kph) tailwind without any problems. Only two unscheduled engine shutdowns had been made in flight, and the revised date for FAA certification of 16 April 1972 was on target.

On 17 May 1971 the third TriStar entered the flight test programme only two days behind the revised schedule, bringing total test flying time to 160 hours. The first overseas flight was made with an Eastern TriStar to the Paris Air Show in June 1971, the total flight time from Palmdale being 12 hours over four legs. Cruising speed across the Atlantic was Mach 0.81 at a height of 33,000ft (10,100m), the take-off from Goose Bay being at a weight of 378,000lb (172,000kg); Shannon was reached four hours later. The RB211 engines were now reaching at least 42,000lb (187kN) thrust, while some were achieving 46,000lb (204kN), and the quietness of the engines was particularly impressive. After leaving Paris the TriStar called at East Midlands airport near Derby in the UK, to be viewed by Rolls-Royce employees.

By 25 June the three TriStars in the flight development programme had made 109 flights with a maximum speed of Mach 0.91, and a maximum altitude of 37,500ft (11,500m) had been achieved. Maximum indicated airspeed of 440kts (815kph) had been registered below 22,000ft (6,700m). Twenty nine automatic landings had been made and 35 pilots from actual or potential airline operators had sampled the TriStar. Flutter testing had found no problems in any part of the flight envelope. The engines had continued to operate effectively, with 20 flight-rated engines delivered to Lockheed, eight of which were developing more than 40,000lb (178kN) thrust.

By mid-July the engines had logged over 1,000 flight hours on the TriStar, and with 42,000lb (187kN) of thrust being achieved, the aircraft was able to investigate performance limitations, reaching the design altitude of 42,000ft (12,800m), and the maximum design speed of 660mph (1,060kph) or Mach 0.95 in a shallow dive from 40,000ft (12,200m). Noise measurements taken during the first eight months of flight testing showed that the engines would be substantially quieter than the noise standards laid down, giving 60 to 70 percent less noise than the aircraft types the TriStar would be replacing in service.

The automatic landing programme had progressed well with over 40 autolands made by the end of July, and the three test aircraft had flown about 420 hours. With the political and economic problems solved in September, the flight testing began to progress well with exploration of the flight performance envelope being taken sometimes beyond the normal design limits, to provide adequate margin for flutter clearance, Mach 0.958 being reached on one flight.

By the end of September 1971, production of the engines was building up rapidly with the 42,000lb (187kN) engines flying in the second aircraft and more than 85 percent of the parts made for the first airline service engines.

Before the fourth TriStar flew on 24 October 1971, it was used by the FAA for engineering analysis as part of the certification process. The certification flight testing became a major part of the programme from 16 November until completion in April 1972. The fifth and final TriStar in the test programme flew on 2 December, just as the flight development programme had passed the halfway mark towards the planned 1,700 hours. This was one of two aircraft allocated to Eastern a month prior to certification for crew training followed by route proving. By October two of the flight test TriStars had RB211 engines developing 42,000lb (187kN), with deliveries achieving a ship-set of three engines every 10 days. The flight testing was now ahead of schedule with all the airline guarantees being met or exceeded, and with component replacement times reduced by 40 percent from the targets set three years previously.

The provisional airworthiness certificate was issued by the FAA for the TriStar on 27 December 1971, two months ahead of the revised schedule, allowing route proving and demonstration flying on non-revenue operations. By the end of 1971 parts' construction and subassembly of the 51st TriStar had commenced at Burbank and assembly of the 22nd aircraft had commenced at Palmdale. The sixth and seventh TriStars were due for roll-out in January 1972 to be allocated to Eastern and TWA for crew training to start. The TriStar icing trials had proved the satisfactory operation of the ice protection system, flying for a total of 24 hours in icing conditions at altitudes of between 10,000 and 20,000ft (3,000–6,100m) up the West Coast of the USA and Canada as far north as Alaska.

All 18 engines for the flight development programme had been delivered and in early January 1972 the RB211 engine was declared ready for operations with no new failures recorded. Deliveries of the engines were a few weeks behind schedule, but this was due to production being ahead of the modifications' programme. In addition to the flight testing of the engines, two RB211s were run on the Derby testbeds in Britain on the 150-hour type test, including 20 hours at full power. One engine was operated at the cold day thrust of 45,000lb (200kN) and the other on a simulated 22°C day thrust of 38,000lb (169kN).

By early February 1972 the TriStar test fleet had accumulated nearly 1,300 flight hours of the total of 1,670 required by the FAA for certification, and the British Air Registration Board (ARB) team had started its certification programme. Tests had included a high energy rejected take-off at the maximum take-off weight of 430,000lb (195,000kg), and premature take-offs were made by scraping the protected rear fuselage along the runway to ensure it would not be able to stall during the take-off run. On the fatigue test specimen 12,500 flights had been simulated — equivalent to 10 years' airline service — and the static test airframe had survived even with critical structural members cut to simulate damage.

A provisional ARB certification was issued to the engine on 24 February 1972, allowing route proving and demonstrations to start; British and American certification took place on 22 March. This was as a result of the successful 150-hour test run at maximum operating temperature, followed by an engine strip and inspection. This cleared the RB211 for passenger operations at an initial thrust of 42,000lb (187kN) with performance improvements in hand by the end of the year.

By this time one RB211 engine was being produced every working day, with 140 due for delivery by the end of the year. By closing 52 sites Rolls-Royce had reduced manpower by 9,500 people and floor space by one million square feet, resolving its financial problems. The RB211 had been cleared of its earlier technical problems and formed the basis for a world-beating competitive engine.

On 15 April 1972 the TriStar was awarded its FAA type certificate, some five months later than originally planned, enabling Eastern Airways and TWA to commence passenger operations. This delay proved not to be serious as, with the reduced passenger demand of the time, the airlines had adequate capacity, and early delivery of the TriStars would have meant more empty seats being flown. The TriStar was the first aircraft to have Cat 3a automatic landing included in its initial certification, allowing landings with a 650ft (200m) cloudbase and a runway visual range (RVR) of 700ft (210m). As well as having many advanced features, which are still appreciated today, the TriStar was also the quietest commercial jet airliner at the time, with noise levels of 98EPNdB for take-off, 95 for side-line and 103 on the approach, as compared with the certification limits of 105.6, 107 and 107EPNdB respectively. On a logarithmic scale these were considerably quieter than required.

British type certification of the TriStar followed in July 1972 after around 30 hours of test flying by the ARB; these concentrated particularly on the autoland capabilities of the aircraft. Because of the close work of the ARB with the manufacturer and the FAA, very little additional work needed to be done to comply with the British requirements.

The TriStar and RB211 engine had therefore survived the economic challenges of their design and development, achieving all their technical goals ready to start recovering the costs in commercial service.

PROBLEMS

The high costs involved not only in launching a new aircraft but a new engine as well, can be very challenging, especially when both are major steps into new technology and scales of operation. The TriStar programme became well known for the financial troubles that almost brought down Lockheed and did result in the bankruptcy of Rolls-Royce. What made things worse was that both the aircraft and engine were launched at a time of high inflation and a downturn in the world economy resulting in a slackening in demand for airline passenger seats. The highly competitive market resulted in very keen and uneconomic prices being quoted for airline equipment in the hope of gaining a position in the marketplace which could later be exploited. However, the stage was reached where the production of the aircraft and engines could not be financed out of existing sales, requiring expensive borrowing to survive. The gamble eventually paid off for the restructured Rolls-Royce but Lockheed had to write off considerable funds and terminate TriStar production earlier than it would have liked, taking the company out of the commercial airliner business.

In 1968 Lockheed made a profit of $44 million (£18.5 million), but the growing costs of the TriStar development programme caused losses of $32.5 million (£13.58 million) the following year. Such a loss would not normally be too serious a problem if the company had a number of other profitable programmes in hand, but for Lockheed at this time, this was not the case. The other programmes contributing to the overall loss were:

- The C-5A Galaxy heavy lift transport for the USAF. Being built to a fixed price contract, it was subject to cost overruns of around $2,000 million (£834 million), because of a reduction in the size of the original contract and structural problems with the wings.
- The cancellation of the Cheyenne helicopter by the US Army had cost Lockheed up to $110 million.
- There were cost overruns with the Short Range Attack Missile and a number of US Navy contracts.

Despite Lockheed being the largest US defence contractor, it could not sustain these losses, and on 2 March 1970 the company chairman requested that the US Government make $640 million (£267 million) in advanced payments to save the company from financial crisis.

The urgent need was for an improvement in short-term cashflow, as only the four disputed programmes were in need of finance, while the company had a number of successful programmes in hand worth some $500 million (£209 million) of future orders. The US Government therefore had the choice of renegotiating the difficult programmes in the interests of national defence, perhaps creating an unwelcome precedent, or the perhaps less attractive alternatives of a company reorganisation, merger or liquidation, the latter resulting in a total loss of all the current programmes and the vast sums invested in them, as well as major job losses which would result.

Meanwhile, in Britain the first hint of financial troubles with Rolls-Royce was beginning to show. At that time the sole user of the RB211 engine was the TriStar. Not only had development costs been increased by inflation, but some unexpected technical problems — particularly with the application of carbonfibre materials — had also added to the costs. As a result Rolls-Royce received a loan of £20 million from the British Government-sponsored Industrial Reorganisation Corporation (IRC) in May 1970. Immediately £10 million was made available to help provide the cashflow until a positive income could be generated with later deliveries. However, to remain in the international jet engine market, with competition from Pratt & Whitney and General Electric, Rolls-Royce had been forced to lower its prices to below an economic level in the hope of gaining the profits out of the eventual long-term business. Normally new products can to some extent be financed out of the revenue from existing sales, but in this case the difference in scale was too great. Dart engines sold for £7,000 from 1953; the Spey engine sold for £65,000 from the 1960s in low numbers: both small beer when compared with the RB211 engine whose initial selling price was over £250,000. Not only could such an investment not be financed out of reasonable existing sales, but there was also a need to maintain investment in other engine programmes. The British Government had originally agreed to provide 70 percent of the development costs for the RB211 engine, but this was based on a fixed-cost estimate and did not take account of any increases caused by inflation or technical problems.

In an effort to reduce weight in the new RB211 engine, Rolls-Royce had decided to use carbonfibre fan blades — but it was found that they did not have the structural strength to withstand the critical bird impact test. Heavier titanium blades had to be substituted at additional cost until the problems with the carbonfibre blades could be solved.

In August 1970 Lockheed was able to announce a better than expected half year profit of $8.3 million (£3.5 million), but the C-5A programme was in deep trouble with the possibility that production would cease after only 31 aircraft were completed. This would leave a further 50 uncompleted aircraft in various stages of construction, out of the total order for 115 aircraft. This would result in a $1,000 million (£417 million) loss to the US Government, whereas a $200 million (£84 million) aid package would see the project progress until the TriStar was generating a positive cashflow, when deliveries were to begin at the end of 1971.

When the first TriStar was rolled out on 1 September 1970, the order book appeared healthy with orders accounting for some 80 percent of the planned break-even of 225 aircraft. Some of these commitments were in fact deposit-paid options, still to be confirmed. Lockheed was keen to open up the market prospects by offering a long-range version of the TriStar, as part of a growing family, but the existing power of the RB211 engines was insufficient and Lockheed began considering a version of the General Electric CF6-50 used to power the DC-10-30. However this engine would have offered only modest improvements and involved further unaffordable development costs.

To overcome some of the immediate cashflow problems, Lockheed was able to negotiate a loan of $30 million (£12.5 million) with a consortium of 24 banks, bringing total borrowings to $350 million (£146 million), with a further loan in prospect, if required. To protect their interests, the major launch airlines were making additional advanced payments.

On 11 November 1970 Frederick Corfield, the British Minister of Aviation Supply, announced in the House of Commons that the cost of development of the RB211 engine had risen from its last estimate of £75 million to £135 million, the original estimated cost being £65 million. The Government had therefore decided to provide a further £42 million, in addition to the £47 million originally agreed. On the same day Rolls-Royce announced losses of £48.1 million during the first half of the year, much attributed to the RB211 programme, and as a result Sir Denning Pearson, the Chairman, resigned and was replaced by Lord Cole.

Apart from the technical difficulties with the engine, the major financial penalties were losses against the keenly negotiat-

RIGHT: While attempts were being made to rescue the TriStar programme, the prototype continued with its flight development testing, although on a somewhat reduced scale. *Lockheed*

ed fixed price contract of £180 million covering 600 engines over a five-year period. Although escalation clauses were included in the agreement, they were insufficient to cope with the unexpected high rate of inflation being experienced at the time.

To help make the programme more viable, Lockheed decided to increase the basic cost of the TriStar by four percent, to be effective on orders placed after 1 February 1971. This price increase of $600,000 (£250,000) on the original price of around $15 million (£6.25 million) included a proportion for Rolls-Royce. This was insufficient within the overall scale of the problems; however, a further increase in the price would have put the TriStar out of the market. The US Government felt that Lockheed should be able to sustain losses of $200 million (£83 million) on the C-5A and Cheyenne programmes.

Then, on 4 February 1971, came the financial collapse of Rolls-Royce. With the current estimate of launching costs approaching £170 million, and the cost of producing each of the first 550 engines for Lockheed £110,000 more than the contract price of £350,000, the company was unable to proceed with the RB211. Despite the remainder of the business being profitable, much of the additional promised funding had not been made available, and Rolls-Royce was put into receivership to avoid a possible claim for damages from Lockheed. Uncontrolled inflation, technical problems and the resultant late deliveries had all conspired towards bringing about the collapse.

The loss of the resources already committed to the RB211 programme combined with the termination costs were expected to exceed the net tangible assets of the company making it insolvent. The assets essential to the defence of Britain, to overseas air forces, world airlines and international collaborative programmes were acquired by the British Government, while the continuation of the RB211 programme was to be assessed. Meanwhile necessary work continued on the engines to keep options open for a renegotiated contract with Lockheed and its customers.

Lockheed called a briefing meeting with its customers in New York on 9 February, but there was very little to report so soon, especially as the future of the RB211 programme was so ill defined. Lockheed was pressing for the future of the engine to be assured by 26 February, as it was suffering unacceptable financial exposure, but this was not sufficient time for the assessment to be completed.

Meanwhile legislation enabling the British Government to purchase the assets of Rolls-Royce received full Parliamentary approval on 15 February, but without any commitment to the RB211 engine. The new company, known as Rolls-Royce (1971) Ltd, was registered on 23 February as a new nationalised company, managed by a new nine-man board of directors headed by Lord Cole. Dan Houghton, the Chairman of Lockheed, began talks with the new board in early March, while work in progress continued on the RB211 underwritten by the British Government. One of the proposals by the British Government was that a joint company be set up with Lockheed to manage the remaining development and production of the engines.

Britain would invest yet a further £60 million, if Lockheed would undertake to finance the balance, although estimates varied as to how much it would cost to deliver engines to a standard acceptable to the airlines. Lord Carrington, the British Minister of Defence, also required guarantees covering the entire British contribution from Lockheed should that company or the TriStar programme collapse.

As the financial investigation progressed, the news did not become any better. Not only were the research and development costs still increasing, but the unit price of each engine had risen to between £150,000 and £190,000 more than the contracted price, bringing in more than a 50 percent loss on every engine sold. At this point the alternatives of the Pratt & Whitney and General Electric engines were becoming attractive with their development costs at $50 million (£21 million). Also the delivery delays of the RB211 gave no real advantage to Rolls-Royce, reducing the negotiating position of the British Government. The airline customers were reluctant to cancel the

TriStar in favour of the DC-10, as they stood to lose their own investment in the programme, but General Electric could afford to buy into the TriStar programme with its CF6 large fan engine. Meanwhile the delivery of RB211 engines continued to Lockheed to sustain the flight development programme.

As an insurance, Delta Airlines — an early TriStar customer — announced its order for five DC-10s with options on a further three on 18 March. The TriStar contract remained, with advanced payments of $34 million (£14.2 million), which was considerably less than the Eastern and TWA commitments. Negotiations continued in Washington DC between Rolls-Royce and Lockheed with direct access to the relevant government departments in Britain and the USA, the aim being to come to an agreement as soon as possible. Lord Carrington, the chief British negotiator, was reported to have doubled the British contribution of engine development to £120 million, but the US Government refused to provide guarantees to cover British expenditure should Lockheed be declared bankrupt.

Finally, at the end of March, a conditional agreement was reached on the new unit price of the RB211 engines, but the actual figure remained confidential until Lockheed had renegotiated with its customers. The agreement did not involve a joint company; however, if it was successful, it would not only ensure the future of the RB211 engine, but Rolls-Royce as well.

The Lockheed negotiations included the airlines, the consortium of 24 banks and the US Treasury to secure an additional $150 million (£63 million), in addition to the $350 million (£144 million) already made available. The US Government proposed a loan guarantee to the banking consortium to cover $250 million (£104 million) in loans to support the TriStar, provided there was approval from Congress. The airlines were expected to provide a further $100 million (£42 million) in down payments, but although Lockheed was becoming more stable, production had come to a halt because of late deliveries of the engines, and many of the employees were laid off.

A statement from the British Government on 10 May gave

hard and fast date for Rolls-Royce, as by then much of the additional £100 million development money would be committed. On 8 June agreement was reached between Lockheed and the Pentagon that losses on the C-5A programme should be limited to $200 million, with the USAF agreeing to cover the remaining costs of producing the full order for the aircraft. In an effort to avoid objections by the US Government to a specific rescue of Lockheed, the proposals were put along the lines of providing support for any company in difficulty which may have a serious effect on the national economy. In many cases it was not expected to cost the US tax payer anything, as the government was only providing guarantees to the banks. The Pentagon believed that Lockheed would need to sell 350 TriStars to break even, but the company's estimate was a break even at around 260 sales, and it did not see any problem in repaying the guaranteed loans.

The House of Representatives gave its approval to the Refinance Bill on 30 July, which covered the assistance to Lockheed only and not the wider industrial coverage, with the Senate vote to follow before the 8 August deadline, as well as the Senate summer recess. Six months of uncertainty was ended on 2 August, when the Senate voted in favour of the $250 million (£105 million) guarantee specifically for Lockheed, allowing the TriStar programme to continue. The British Government extended its financial support until 24 August to allow confirmation of the Lockheed/Rolls-Royce contract, and also to allow the remaining airline customers to agree to the price increases. Negotiations continued with the US Treasury to finalise details of the loan guarantee, which was valid until the end of 1973, by which time the debt was expected to have been paid off, and on 9 September formal US Government approval was given, allowing the new contracts to be signed. Final settlement was reached on 14 September 1971, allowing the TriStar programme to start again at full capacity.

The final agreement had been reached in a complex financial package involving two governments, two major aerospace companies and a group of major international airlines. Lockheed avoided bankruptcy by a close margin and Rolls Royce was saved by the British Government, later returning to private ownership, and continuing to develop the RB211 engine family world-wide.

some preliminary details of the agreement with Lockheed, confirming financial support for the engine throughout its life, providing the TriStar obtained full support. Lockheed had made concessions by waiving penalties for late deliveries, and had agreed to an increase in the unit cost of the engine of £46,000, bringing in an additional £50 million over the first 555 engines. On 12 May the new contract was signed for the supply of engines to Lockheed, conditional upon the US Congressional approval of the proposed loan guarantees. The Lockheed financial plan to continue the TriStar programme was estimated to require $750 million (£315 million), with $400 million (£168 million) already loaned, a further $250 million (£105 million) to be loaned and guaranteed by the US Government and $100 million (£42 million) in additional advanced payments from the airlines. At the end of May, Lockheed announced a $86.3 million (£35.9 million) loss for 1970, largely due to the increased commitment to the TriStar.

The British Government had set 8 August as its deadline for the agreement, but dropped the unacceptable condition that the US Government should provide compensation should the TriStar programme collapse. The 8 August deadline was not a

3 PRODUCTION

PRODUCTION LOCATIONS

Early on in the TriStar programme, the decision was made to build a new factory capable of handling the planned production rate for the perceived market. If this had not been done at the start, Lockheed would have been unable to cope with the required levels of production, and would have therefore been incompetitive. In reality, it was also one of the main reasons for Lockheed's high financial loss with the TriStar, because the cost of the production tooling and facilities could not be recovered over only 250 aircraft. The new, purpose-designed, manufacturing facility, Plant 10, was constructed at Palmdale, California on 677 acres: Lockheed's 'Star Factory in the Desert', cost over $50 million (£21 million). The seven-building complex was designed specifically to incorporate the most advanced concepts in aircraft production and logistical support. The location was also ideal from the point of view of weather, allowing much of the work to be done outside, and almost uninterrupted flight testing.

The main assembly building had a floor space of nearly 1.3 million square feet (120,770sq m) under one roof, employing some 6,000 people during peak production. If the demand had required, production could have reached up to 10 TriStars a month, with the major parts produced at Burbank and final assembly and flight testing at Palmdale. This vast new facility took two years of major civil engineering activity starting with a virgin desert site. The materials, sub-assemblies and equipment for the TriStar were delivered to the factory by road, air and rail — a special rail spur being laid into it. In the main factory, the floor was split into two key areas: fuselage assembly on one side and assembly of the aircraft themselves on a double track on the other. The first aircraft was actually built inside the new factory as facility itself was being constructed. The building was dedicated by Ronald Reagan, then the Governor of the State of California, on 20 July 1970.

BELOW: The TriStar prototype N1011 was reconfigured in the mid-1970s as a test vehicle for the proposed new technologies including extended wing span and active ailerons. It is seen here flying over the Palmdale Factory in the desert. *Lockheed*

CONSTRUCTION

Every new aircraft requires a massive investment in time, skill and money in new jigs and tools, often causing greater challenges than building the aircraft themselves. All the major jigs and tools were produced by the Lockheed craftsmen at Burbank, the large fuselage panels requiring major new jigs. In such a large new aircraft, care has to be taken to keep weight growth down, while retaining structural strength. With the fuselage panels, new fabrication techniques had to be developed, the side walls being semi-monocoque shells with tapered frames and thicker skins, reducing the need for stringers. Not only did this help reduce weight, but also it cut down on manufacturing time. The double curvature fuselage skins, some up to 15ft (4.6m) wide and 38ft (11.7m) long, were formed over stretcher presses; strengthening panels, to improve fatigue life and corrosion resistance, were bonded on in the largest autoclaves in the aerospace industry. The bonding process avoided the need to rivet and bolt components together, providing a lighter, stronger joint.

Lockheed used conventional metals with the TriStar structure since the use of composites — as is current today — had not been developed sufficiently then to provide a certifiable standard as far as any major structural members were concerned. However, as with all the new generation of wide-bodied jet airliners, great care had to be taken to keep structural weight to a minimum: if it had increased in the same proportion as the size of the aircraft itself increased, the project would have been significantly overweight. One of the methods of providing a lighter and stronger structure was to use metal-to-metal bonding, as described above, This gives a very strong joint and, as there are no holes for rivets and bolts to weaken the skins, thinner gauge metals can be used.

The fuselages were painted before final assembly in the third largest building in the Palmdale complex. The aim was to produce a higher quality finish in a carefully controlled environment, the aircraft then progressing down the line in full customer livery. It took 40 minutes to apply the 58 gallons (220 litres) of polyurethane paint to the 178ft (54m) long fuselage.

RIGHT: **Five TriStars were used in the flight development programme at Palmdale, the fifth joining the fleet on 2 December 1971. A sixth TriStar, the first service delivery for Eastern, awaits its first flight. The Palmdale factory is in the background.** *Lockheed*

BELOW RIGHT: **The fatigue test airframe at Palmdale was subjected to the equivalent of 36,000 simulated flights under all extremes of airline operation.** *Lockheed*

BELOW: **Three TAP Air Portugal TriStar 500s on the production line — including CS-TEC, c/n 1241, and CS-TED, c/n 1242, which were delivered in March and June of 1983 respectively.** *Lockheed*

ABOVE: Fabrication of the first TriStar commenced at Palmdale in early 1969, while the factory was itself still under construction. Here the Burbank-built canopy is lowered on to the cockpit nose. *Lockheed*

ABOVE LEFT: Rear pressure dome installation. *Lockheed*

LEFT: To keep structural weight to a minimum, the fuselage was built up using thicker gauge skins over tapered frames, avoiding the need for stringers. This also reduced manufacturing time and costs. *Lockheed*

RIGHT: Selecting fuselage frames. *Lockheed*

The tail surfaces were painted separately before assembly. The aircraft then went into final assembly and equipping before its production flight test, following which the aircraft went back into the paint shop for the wings to be painted and any tidying up necessary to the fuselage. Another way weight was controlled was by ensuring that the final painting of the aircraft was carefully monitored. Too much paint could cause a loss of payload, while too little provided insufficient protection against corrosion. The painting of the TriStar was, therefore, monitored by the use of computers to ensure exactly the right thickness.

The purpose-built plant could handle up to 39 TriStars in the assembly jigs, final assembly and flight test at any one time, and at full capacity a TriStar could have been delivered every two days.

To achieve the high standards of production, there had to be a significant investment in tooling, to ensure a high level of interchangeability for spares and repairs, as well as ensuring identical standards of the airframe, engines and equipment. All the aircraft had to perform similarly to achieve a certificate of airworthiness (C of A), which is why, after a rigorous flight development programme leading to the C of A for the type, each production aircraft had to be checked against the agreed standard before delivery to an airline.

In addition to the comprehensive flight development programme, many duplicate parts had to be produced for structural testing, including two full-size airframes for static and dynamic endurance testing, well ahead of the flying aircraft. In addition to these full-scale airframes, all the other major structural assemblies had to be individually tested on the ground, before the aircraft took to the air. While the running of the early development engines on the testbed is perhaps the most obvious example, others include representative drop tests with the undercarriage units, and a full scale 'Iron Bird' ground-based systems test rig which tested the operation and service life of the many systems, to ensure that they would not fail prematurely, and that they were compatible with each other. A generator or hydraulic pump does not know that it is not flying when being tested on the systems rig, but they will be subjected to realistic loads, particularly when a failure is simulated.

PARTNERS

One of the major challenges for all three US West Coast aircraft manufacturers was that, as they were all launching major airliner programmes at the same time, there would be competition for capacity amongst the suppliers of specialist materials and equipment, as well as the major subcontractors. Enquiries were not just limited to the USA. Lockheed also talked to European suppliers, but the first contract was with Avco Aerostructures in Nashville, Tennessee for the TriStar wing structure.

RIGHT: The TriStar fuselages were assembled on one side of the vast assembly hall, painted at one end, and then joined a double track final assembly line, where the Avco-produced wings were attached. This is LTU's D-AERA, which was delivered in June 1973. *Lockheed*

Avco Aerostructures already had a wide experience working with Lockheed on the wings for the C-130 Hercules, the C-141 Starlifter and the massive structures for the C-5A. The contract for the TriStar wings was worth $575 million (£242 million) and involved over 350 wing sets, each wing being 88ft (27m) long, and 24ft (7.3m) wide at the root, tapering down to 4ft (1.2m) wide at the tip. Avco delivered the first TriStar wing to Palmdale by Super Guppy on 27 April 1970, followed a few days later by the other wing. By the end of 1971, a total of 17 wingsets had been delivered from the new Avco purpose-built facility, although by then they were being transported directly into the factory by rail.

Passenger and cargo doors were built by Kawasaki in Japan; from Canada, Northwest Industries produced the pressure bulkhead and floor structures and Bristol Aerospace built the centre engine intake duct. In the USA the wing flaps were built by Aeronca and the engine support pylons were manufactured by Murdock Engineering. The demanding and specialist task of manufacturing the undercarriage units was done by Menasco; the wheels, brakes and tyres came from Goodrich and the anti-skid system was from Goodyear. The flight control system was standardised on Collins equipment, and Sperry supplied the air data computer. Lockheed was responsible for the remainder of the airframe, as well as final assembly.

To help share the massive financial burden, many of the major subcontractors and equipment suppliers were also risk-sharing partners, the most important being Rolls-Royce with its all-new RB211 engines. The TriStar programme was a vital step for the future survival of Rolls-Royce, as it ensured it remained in the major league international jet engine suppliers working with the new large fan engines. However, as we have seen earlier, there are drawbacks to a risk-sharing approach: Rolls-Royce's financial difficulties almost brought the whole project to a premature and untimely end.

It was not only the airframe manufacturers who were moving into a new advanced technology with the wide-bodied jet

ABOVE: The production line at Derby in September 1972. At the time Rolls-Royce was claiming 42,000lb (187kN) take-off thrust for the engines on the line and was predicting a 45,000lb (200kN) version to enter service in spring 1975. *Rolls-Royce*

LEFT: Installing an RB211-22B into a test bed at Rolls-Royce's Derby works. *Rolls-Royce*

RIGHT: Ground crew perform preflight checks on an RB211 at Palmdale, during the flight test programme leading to the TriStar's certification in April 1972. This aircraft is in Eastern Airlines colours and was the first with an airline interior. It was exhibited at the 1971 Paris Air Show. *Lockheed*

airliners: engine manufacturers were having to take a giant step from the traditional noisy and thirsty jet engines, to the new generation of economic and much quieter large fan-engines.

Detail design of the RB211 engine for the TriStar commenced in July 1967 featuring a by-pass ratio of 5:1, the engine core driving a large fan, which acted like a multi-blade propeller, driving some 70 percent of the thrust around the outside of the core. Normally the engine would have two concentric shafts, but the RB211 had three shafts, one driving the fan, and the other two driving their own turbines. This resulted in 25 percent fewer parts to generate the required thrust and the achievement of a high pressure and bypass ratio with a 25 percent improvement in fuel economy. The reduction in overall engine speed,

due to the momentum of the greater volume of air also reduced engine noise. Indeed, the RB211, despite its chequered beginnings, turned out to be a fine engine which would go on to power many other aircraft, including Boeing's 747.

The engines were built at Rolls-Royce's main production and development factories at Derby. Ground test facilities were initially conducted at the nearby test airfield of Hucknall. Later, however, the main flight-testing was carried out at the more suitable airfield at Filton; Hucknall would subsequently close as a flight test centre.

BELOW: As a flight test vehicle for the early RB211 engines, Rolls-Royce modified an ex-RAF VC-10, replacing the pair of Conway engines on the port side with a TriStar representative installation. Formerly XR809 with No 10 Squadron, the aircraft was delivered to Hucknall in April 1969, becoming G-AXLR, and first flew with the RB211 on 6 March 1970. On completion of the flight development programme from Hucknall and Filton, it was retired to No 5 MU at Kemble in October 1975, later being scrapped. *Rolls-Royce*

4 TECHNICAL SPECIFICATION

	L1011-1	L1011-50	L1011-100	L1011-150
Powerplant (3 Rolls-Royce)	RB211-22B	RB211-22B	RB211-22B	RB211-22B
Thrust (lb/kN)	42,000/187	42,000/187	42,000/187	42,000/187
Wingspan (ft in/m)	155ft 4in/47.35	155ft 4in/47.35	155ft 4in/47.35	155ft 4in/47.35
Length (ft in/m)	177ft 8in/54.2	177ft 8in/54.2	177ft 8in/54.2	177ft 8in/54.2
Height (ft in/m)	55ft 4in/18.88	55ft 4in/18.88	55ft 4in/18.88	55ft 4in/18.88
Wing area (sq ft/sq m)	3,456/321.5	3,456/321.5	3,456/321.5	3,456/321.5
Wing sweep,1/4 chord	35°	35°	35°	35°
Max seating	400	400	400	400
Cargo vol (cu ft/cu m)	3,900/110.4	3,900/110.4	3,900/110.4	3,900/110.4
T/O weight (lb/kg)	430,000/195,044	450,000/204,000	466,000/211,374	470,000/213,000
Landing weight (lb/kg)	358,000/162,386	368,000/166,922	368,000/166,922	368,000/166,922
Fuel (Imp Gal/litres/lb)	19,636/89,267/ 160,000	19,636/89,267/ 160,000	21,998/100,000/ 178,000	19,636/89,267/ 160,000
Max cruise @ 33,000 ft(kt)	512	512	512	512
Max payload/range (lb/nm)	83,270/2,950	83,270/2,950	73,534/4,030	73,534/4,030

	L1011-200	L1011-250	L1011-500
Powerplant (3 Rolls-Royce)	RB211-524B	RB211-524B	RB211-524B
Thrust (lb/kN)	50,000/222	50,000/222	50,000/222
Wingspan (ft in/m)	155ft 4in/47.35	155ft 4in/47.35	164ft 4in/50.09
Length (ft in/m)	177ft 8in/54.2	177ft 8in/54.2	164ft 2in/50.04
Height (ft in/m)	55ft 4in/18.88	55ft 4in/18.88	55ft 4in/18.88
Wing area (sq ft/sq m)	3,456/321.5	3,456/321.5	3,537/329
Wing sweep,1/4 chord	35°	35°	35°
Max seating	400	400	333
Cargo vol (cu ft/cu m)	3,900/110.4	3,900/110.4	4,235/119.9
T/O weight (lb/kg)	466,000/211,374	496,000/231,332	482,385/224,982
Landing weight (lb/kg)	368,000/166,922	368,000/166,922	368,000/166,922
Fuel (Imp Gal/litres/lb)	21,998/100,000/ 178,000	26,347/119,776/ 213,600	26,347/119,776/ 213,600
Max cruise @ 33,000 ft(kt)	518	518	518
Max payload/range (lb/nm)	71,415/4,260	88,240/4,850	92,253/4,580

TRISTAR SPECIFICATION

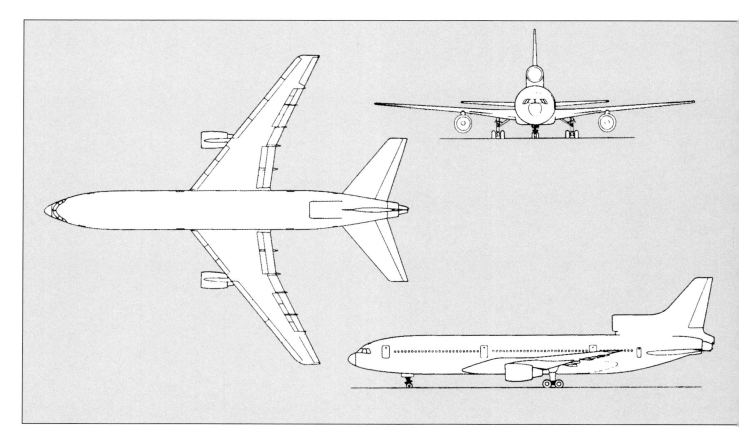

INBOARD PROFILE

FLIGHT
COMPARTMENT

ENVIRONMENTAL
CONTROL
SYSTEM

MAIN
CABIN

AFT ELECTRONICS
EQUIPMENT AREA

RADOME
NOSE

NOSE
LANDING
GEAR WHEEL
WELL

BELOW-
DECK
GALLEY

WING
CENTER
SECTION

CENTER
CARGO
HOLD

AFT
CARGO
HOLD

FORWARD
ELECTRONICS
SERVICE
CENTER

FORWARD
CARGO
HOLD

MID
ELECTRICAL
SERVICE
CENTER

HYDRAULICS
SERVICE
CENTER
AND MAIN
LANDING
GEAR
WHEEL WELLS

FUSELAGE
TAIL SECTION
AND
AUXILIARY
POWER UNIT
AREA

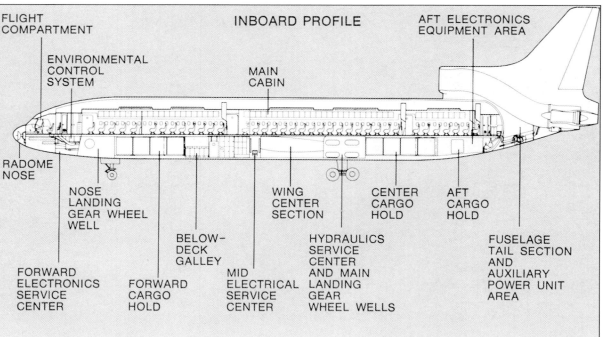

ABOVE: Three-view of the L1011-1. *Lockheed*

LEFT: Inboard profile o the L1011-1. The forward and centre cargo holds were equipped for mechanised container loading and each could take up to eight LD3 containers. The rear hold could take up to 700cu ft (19.8cu m) of bulk loading. *Lockheed*

BELOW LEFT: This side view of the Jordanian Royal Flight's JY-HKJ shows off the clean lines of the L1011-500. This aircraft is a regular visitor to Britain, especially Cambridge Airport, where it is maintained. *Marshall Aerospace*

TOP: Air Canada TriStar 100 C-FTNK on turn-round at Manchester Airport. Note the position of its wide-open cargo hold doors showing access to forward, centre and rear holds. C-FTNK flew its last service with the airline on October 1990, and has now been acquired by the Canadian charter operator, Royal. *Paul Francis*

ABOVE: Delta TriStar 1 N1732D, on approach to Orlando in August 1988, showing the flap position for landing and landing gear extended. *Philip Birtles*

LEFT: Air Transat C-FTNC giving another view of flaps and landing gear. Delivered as N315EA in January 1973 it served with Eastern and Air Canada over the next 10 years before leasing to Air Transat. *Leo Marriott*

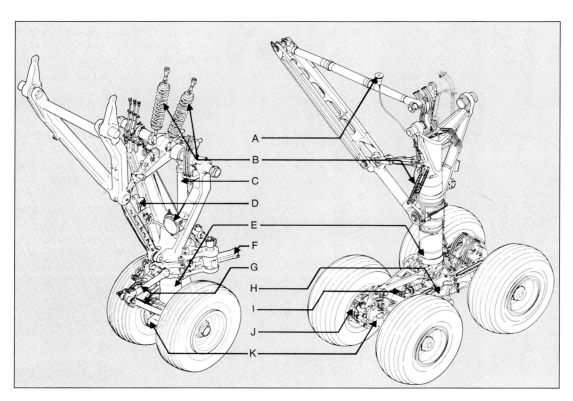

LEFT: The TriStar's fully retractable tricycle-configured landing gear consists of left and right wing-mounted dual tandem wheels and a steerable nose gear assembly. The main landing gear retracts into the fuselage and the nose gear goes into a forward well. There are two identical braking systems — normal and backup — plus a separate accumulator for each system to ensure instant braking action. The brakes themselves are hydraulically actuated multiple disc brakes, whose temperatures are monitored individually by the flight engineer. *Lockheed*

A Visual downlock indicator.
B Downlock springs.
C Retract actuator.
D Taxi lights.
E Shock strut assembly.
F Steering actuators.
G Torque arms.
H Bogie beam.
I Bogie positioner.
J Brake assembly.
K Towing pads.

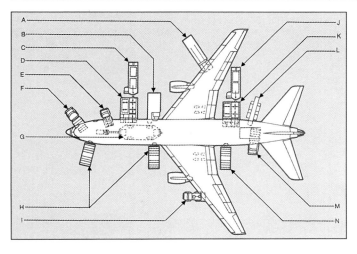

ABOVE AND LEFT: The servicing and passenger loading/unloading facilities are shown in this photograph and drawing. Separate centres are supplied for avionic, electrical, hydraulic and environmental control systems. Lavatories are serviced externally and the below-deck galley is serviced through a separate door removed from the passenger boarding areas. Tow-bar attachments are provided on front and back sides of the nose gear and a low-profile tow tractor can manoeuvre directly under the fuselage to position the aircraft correctly. *Lockheed*

A Fuel tanker.
B Galley service truck.
C Transporter.
D Containerised cargo loader.
E Electrical truck.
F Lavatory truck.
G Tow tractor (low profile).
H Passenger loading stands.
I Hydrant truck.

J Transporter.
K Containerised cargo loader.
L Bulk cargo loader.
M Lavatory truck.
N Passenger loading stand.

Auxiliary power unit provisions:
• electrical power
• engine starting air
• air conditioning

ABOVE LEFT: Inside the cockpit — captain (left) and first officer concentrate on finals. As the clothing indicates, this is actually a test-flight out of Palmdale and not an airline operation. *Lockheed*

ABOVE: An EFIS — electronic flight instrument systems — cockpit was installed in the development prototype. It looks very different to that installed on the service TriStar, with LEDs taking the place of many of the dials (compare with picture on next page). *Lockheed*

LEFT: Flight engineer's console and instrumentation. *Lockheed*

Flightdeck

The TriStar is normally operated by a crew of three, the captain, first officer and flight engineer. The captain sits in the left-hand seat, with the first officer on the right, and the flight engineer at his systems desk behind the first officer. While the two pilots are responsible for the flight operation of the aircraft, the flight engineer ensures that all the systems are functioning, including fuel flow to the engines, air-conditioning and pressurisation for the comfort of all on board, and also monitors the flight crew workload during the busy times of flight, such as take-off and landing. A fourth seat on the flightdeck, behind the captain, is for any additional crew member — for example a training captain who may be involved with the competency checking of the operating crew, or just another crew member returning home after an outbound trip.

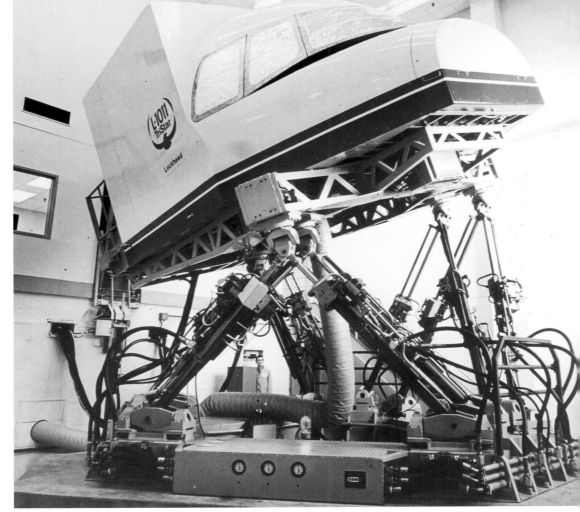

RIGHT: The Lockheed L1011 flight simulator duplicates all the normal flight attitudes, reducing the cost of pilot training. Note the hydraulic jacks. *Lockheed*

BELOW: The flight simulator cockpit duplicates exactly the conditions in the usual TriStar cockpit. At right, the flight engineer's console (for detail of his instrumentation see previous page). *Lockheed*

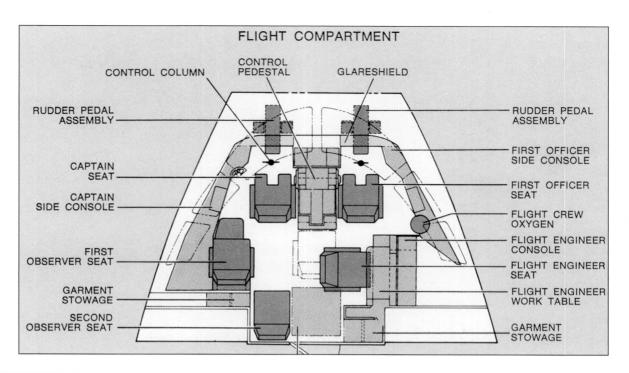

FLIGHT COMPARTMENT

CONTROL COLUMN — CONTROL PEDESTAL — GLARESHIELD

RUDDER PEDAL ASSEMBLY

CAPTAIN SEAT

CAPTAIN SIDE CONSOLE

FIRST OBSERVER SEAT

GARMENT STOWAGE

SECOND OBSERVER SEAT

RUDDER PEDAL ASSEMBLY

FIRST OFFICER SIDE CONSOLE

FIRST OFFICER SEAT

FLIGHT CREW OXYGEN

FLIGHT ENGINEER CONSOLE

FLIGHT ENGINEER SEAT

FLIGHT ENGINEER WORK TABLE

GARMENT STOWAGE

RIGHT: Schematic of the flight compartment. While it may look crowded, it has been well designed to allow good visibility — external and internal — and good stowage facilities. The windshield main panels are made of laminated stretched acrylic with a thin outer layer of tempered glass and a hard scratch-resistant chemical coating on the inner surface to give distortion-free viewing for the pilots and good resistance against bird strikes. In an emergency, flightdeck crew exit through an overhead escape hatch. *Lockheed*

ABOVE AND RIGHT: Two early publicity views of cabin seating — that on the right describes the 'fashionable luxury' to welcome first class passengers. *Lockheed*

Cabin

To give the maximum space for the passenger layouts in the main cabin, Lockheed located the galleys below the main floor, providing service by the use of lifts. The remainder of the fuselage underfloor area is allocated to systems in specific areas, and for passenger baggage and cargo. The entire cabin is a pressure shell, with a small bulkhead in front of the flightdeck, and a massive pressure dome at the rear of the cabin, behind the toilets. Each airline has its own special requirements for seating layouts, according to the mix of first, business and economy classes, but the wide-bodied cabin allowed rows of up to eight seats in a twin aisle 2-4-2 configuration.

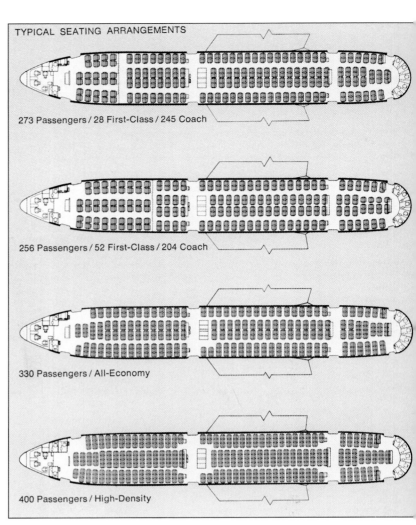

TYPICAL SEATING ARRANGEMENTS

273 Passengers / 28 First-Class / 245 Coach

256 Passengers / 52 First-Class / 204 Coach

330 Passengers / All-Economy

400 Passengers / High-Density

ABOVE: A stewardess awaits the lift to take her from the below-deck galley to the main cabin. The lift arrives at the mid-cabin service centre (see drawing below). *Lockheed*

RIGHT: Various seating arrangements as shown in Lockheed's L1011-1 technical manual. *Lockheed*

LEFT: Trolley service in a TriStar cabin mockup. *Lockheed*

BELOW LEFT: Schematic showing passenger service locations on the TriStar. *Lockheed*

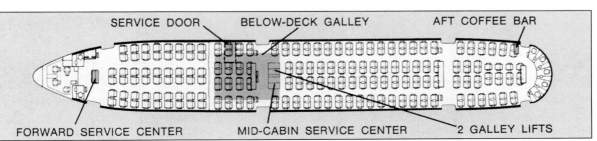

SERVICE DOOR   BELOW-DECK GALLEY   AFT COFFEE BAR

FORWARD SERVICE CENTER   MID-CABIN SERVICE CENTER   2 GALLEY LIFTS

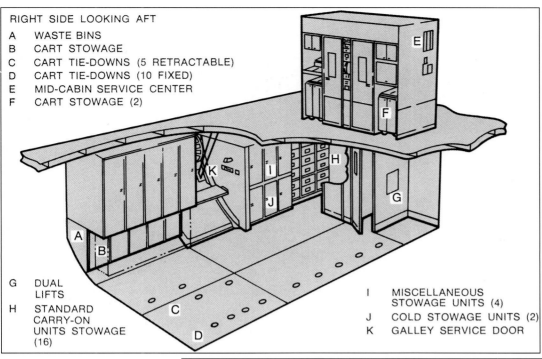

RIGHT SIDE LOOKING AFT

A   WASTE BINS
B   CART STOWAGE
C   CART TIE-DOWNS (5 RETRACTABLE)
D   CART TIE-DOWNS (10 FIXED)
E   MID-CABIN SERVICE CENTER
F   CART STOWAGE (2)

G   DUAL LIFTS
H   STANDARD CARRY-ON UNITS STOWAGE (16)

I   MISCELLANEOUS STOWAGE UNITS (4)
J   COLD STOWAGE UNITS (2)
K   GALLEY SERVICE DOOR

LEFT: Below-deck galley facilities. There is sufficient storage for up to 600 full-course meals — adequate for two-meal service in most interior configurations. *Lockheed*

RIGHT: The other side of the galley. *Lockheed*

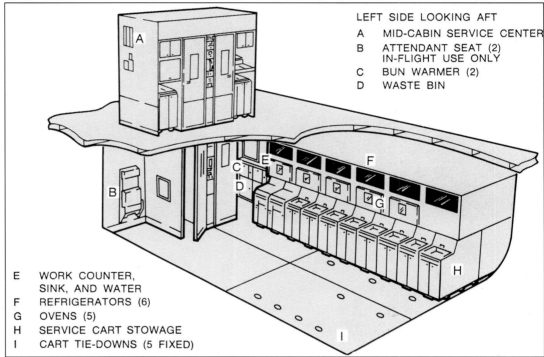

LEFT SIDE LOOKING AFT

A   MID-CABIN SERVICE CENTER
B   ATTENDANT SEAT (2) IN-FLIGHT USE ONLY
C   BUN WARMER (2)
D   WASTE BIN

E   WORK COUNTER, SINK, AND WATER
F   REFRIGERATORS (6)
G   OVENS (5)
H   SERVICE CART STOWAGE
I   CART TIE-DOWNS (5 FIXED)

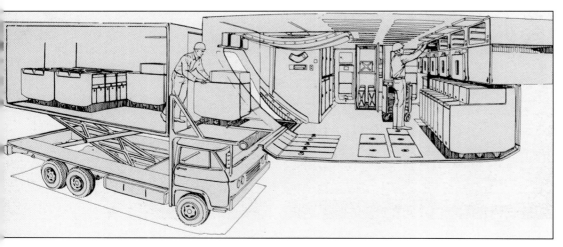

LEFT: A galley door allows servicing concurrent with cargo and passenger loading. *Lockheed*

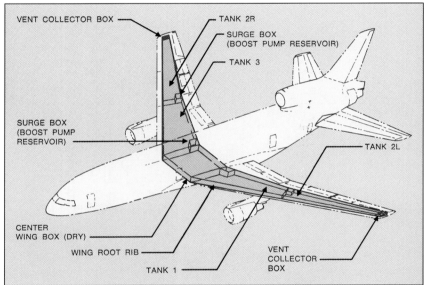

ABOVE: Close-up of the TriStar wing showing leading edge slat and trailing edge flap operation. *Lockheed*

ABOVE RIGHT: Flight control surfaces schematic. There are four independent hydromechanical systems. The flight controls are powered by servo-actuators. *Lockheed*

RIGHT: Fuel tank arrangements. The four integral wing tanks have a capacity of 159,560lb (72,375kg) of fuel. There are two pressure fuelling stations, outboard of each engine nacelle. These can load c100,000lb (c45,500kg) of fuel in 10 minutes. *Lockheed*

Wings

The TriStar wings are known as 'wet wings', each having integral fuel tanks within the sealed structure, as well as in some cases also the wing centre section under the mid-cabin. This provides the greatest capacity for the lowest weight.

Flight systems

The flight systems on the TriStar were designed to be automatic throughout the flight from take-off to touch-down, the pilots being in effect systems' operators for the sophisticated on-board computers.

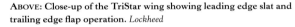

LEFT: The Avionic Flight Control System (AFCS) provides manual or automatic modes of control throughout the total flight envelope from take-off to landing. It has four major subsystems — the autopilot/flight director system, yaw stability augmentation system, speed control system and primary flight control electronic system. These subsystems are integrated to meet stringent safety and performance demands. The schematic opposite shows the AFCS total flight profile capability. *Lockheed*

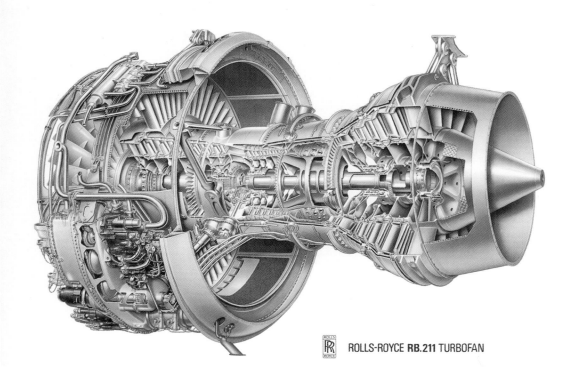

ROLLS-ROYCE **RB.211** TURBOFAN

LEFT: Cutaway of the Rolls-Royce RB211 turbofan. *Rolls-Royce*

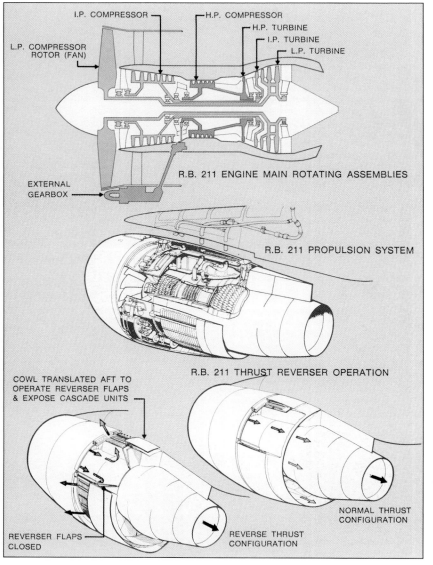

ABOVE: Intake duct for the rear engine. *Leo Marriott*

LEFT: Engine and reverse thrust operation schematics. *Lockheed*

Power and Auxiliary power

Much of the power — electrical and hydraulic — required for the aircraft systems is taken from the engines through generators and pumps. For power on the ground, giving an independence from local services, an auxiliary power unit (APU) is fitted, which is used for the environmental systems in the aircraft interior, when on the ground, whether it is blowing an Arctic blizzard outside, or at a tropical paradise. The APU is a small turbine engine, usually situated in the rear end of the fuselage.

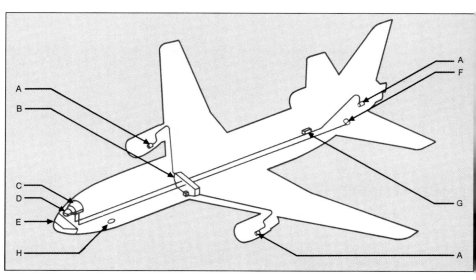

RIGHT: The primary electric power generating system consists of four 90kVA 120/208V ac 400hz generators. Three are engine-driven; the fourth is generated by the APU — the auxiliary power unit. Electrical power system details:
A Integrated drive generator.
B Mid-electrical service centre.
C Circuit breaker panel.
D Overhead control panel.
E Forward electronics service centre.
F APU generator.
G Aft electronics equipment area.
H External power receptacle. *Lockheed*

BELOW: The three-shaft layout of the RB211 engine gives good power response and low vibration levels, and the large front fan gives low noise levels and economy. *Rolls-Royce*

Variants

Lockheed's TriStar programme planned to develop a family of aircraft with a high proportion of common equipment. This would make production more efficient, maintenance more economical and produce a fleet which could cope with a range of airline requirements. The financial problems, made worse by the downturn in the world economy, together with the oil crises, conspired against Lockheed in achieving these ideal goals. However, although the TriStar programme was a financial disaster for the manufacturer, it was technologically very advanced and has always been popular with aircrew, maintenance personnel and passengers, as well as making good returns for the operators.

TriStar developments were mainly concerned with low cost options of extending the range as the power of the RB211 engines increased, allowing the carriage of more fuel. Ideas for long-range versions started in 1969 with the **L1011-8.4** powered by three 52,200lb (232kN) thrust RB211-56 engines, capable of carrying up to 280 passengers over distances of 6,000 miles (9,600km), the take-off weight of 575,000lb (261,000kg) being

supported by a stronger undercarriage. The fuselage would have been stretched by 40in (1.2m) to 182ft 8in (55.7m), and the wing area would be increased by 20 percent. Further growth was announced in January 1970 when the gross weight could be increased by 20,000lb (9,100kg) by taking advantage of the increased thrust of the RB211-56 engines, which were predicted to be capable of developing 53,500lb (238kN). These proposals were shelved because of costs when Lockheed was suffering from its financial problems.

In February 1972, Lockheed proposed the **L1011-2** which would have the same dimensions as the existing aircraft, but with structural strengthening taking the gross weight to 466,000lb (212,000kg) giving a range of 4,000nm (7,400km). Strong efforts were made in 1972 to launch this version to at least three of the existing operators. The BA order for TriStars in August 1972 coincided with British Government approval for the start of development of the RB211-24 engine, costing around £31 million, and suitable for powering the L1011-2. This would give a transatlantic range in all weather conditions, making the aircraft particularly attractive to existing customers. In its production form the engine was designated the RB211-524, having the maximum commonality and interchangeability with the earlier engine. With a service entry scheduled for 1975, the new version of the engine would have an improved fuel consumption with a thrust potentially up to 50,000lb (222kN), achieved by modest refinements to the engine including reduced operating temperatures, an increase in mass flow of the air through the engine and a slight reduction in the by-pass ratio. This engine development was also suitable for the higher capacity L1011-3 as well as the 'BiStar' — an unbuilt proposal for a twin-engined L1011. Other unbuilt proposals included a freighter modified to run on liquid hydrogen, with two fuel tanks installed in a fuselage stretched to its maximum length.

ABOVE: Cathay Pacific TriStar 1 VR-HHY was delivered in July 1978. The L1011-1 was the basic TriStar model. *Cathay Pacific.*

RIGHT: ATA TriStar 50 N190AT at Gatwick. It carries the markings of Pleasant Hawaiian Holidays. The L1011-50 was a conversion package which increased the gross weight to 450,000lb (204,000kg). *Nick Granger*

BELOW: British Airtours TriStar 50 G-BEAM at London Gatwick on 8 December 1985. Originally an L1011-1 it was upgraded to -50 status in March 1985. *Nick Granger*

With the go-ahead of the L1011-2 conditional upon sufficient airline interest, further details were released in April 1973. Maximum take-off weight was increased to 488,000lb (222,000kg) of which some 7,000lb (3,200kg) was accounted for by structural strengthening and additional equipment, giving an increase of 51,000lb (23,200kg) over the basic aircraft. Range at Mach 0.82 was estimated to be 4,000nm (7,400km) while carrying 273 passengers. At this stage the engines were to develop 45,000lb (200kN) of thrust each, but in the following month Rolls-Royce was able to announce a further increase in thrust to 48,000lb (213kN), allowing either 70 more passengers to be carried, or extending the range by 400 miles (650km). The gross weight was also able to grow to 516,000lb (234,000kg). Two versions of the L1011-2 were being considered by Lockheed, one carrying 256 passengers up to 4,600nm (8,500km), and the other for the long thin routes flying up to 216 passengers over distances of 5,400nm (10,000km).

In early 1974, because of the oil crisis, the 4,600nm (8,500km) range L1011-2 was shelved in the short term, Lockheed concentrating on modifying the existing L1011-1 airframe by adding an extra fuel tank between the wing spars in the centre section, increasing the maximum take-off weight to 466,000lb (212,000kg). In the longer term a **L1011-3** with a fuselage length increased by between 20 and 40ft (6–12m) was being considered, but if the existing undercarriage were retained, the footprint pressure would limit the all-up weight to 525,000lb (238,000kg).

ABOVE RIGHT: Now operated by Air Transat, TriStar 150 C-FTNA is seen on lease to Air France in February 1991. The L1011-150 gave the TriStar 1 a number of improvements including increased range and improved maximum take-off weight. C-FTNA was converted from L1011-1 to -150 in May 1989. *Nick Granger*

RIGHT: TWA TriStar 100 N31033 was delivered in December 1981. Improvements to the basic RB211-22B resulted in the TriStar 1 becoming known as the TriStar 100. *Lockheed*

BELOW: PSA TriStar 1 N10114 first flew in July 1974; it was converted to a Srs 100 in April 1979 and sold to Aero Peru. It is seen here performing at the 1974 Farnborough Air Show. *Rolls-Royce*

It was the Saudia order in September 1974 which allowed the launch of the L1011-2, which in production form became the **TriStar 200**, power coming from 48,000lb (213kN) thrust RB211-524 engines, a 50,000lb (222kN) thrust version of which was also being developed for the Boeing 747. Improvements to the basic RB211-22 powered TriStar resulted in the L1011-1 becoming known as the **TriStar 100**. Lockheed announced the **TriStar 250** at the end of 1974. This had its gross weight increased by a further 18,000lb (8,200kg) over the L1011-200, to a total of 484,000lb (220,000kg), the extra weight being taken up with additional fuel capacity to increase the range to 3,500 miles (5,600km). The overall dimensions and power were unchanged.

In the spring of 1975 bench-testing at Rolls-Royce with the RB211-524 was progressing well, with 1,600 hours run including a series of 150-hour endurance tests. First flight test of the engine was expected to start by the end of the year in the TriStar prototype, with certification to be completed on the first Saudia TriStar in mid-1976.

In November 1975 the major long-range **TriStar 500** version was announced by Lockheed, aimed particularly at a BEA requirement for a long-range version for service entry in the early 1980s. The L1011-500 combined the 50,000lb (222kN) thrust engines with the strengthened structure of the L1011-250, but the fuselage was reduced in length by 20ft 2in (6.1m), 15ft (4.6m) being removed from the fuselage ahead of the wing and 5ft 2in (1.6m) behind the trailing edge. By increasing the fuel capacity by 22,000lb (10,000kg) in extra centre-section fuel tanks, the range

was increased to 5,400nm (10,000km) carrying up to 231 passengers. Maximum take-off weight could be increased to 490,000lb (222,500kg), but apart from thicker skins, the wing was unchanged at this early stage. This provided an aircraft which could effectively replace the Boeing 707 or McDonnell Douglas DC-8 on the long thin routes, as the L1011-250 was a little short on the desired range at 4,200nm (7,800km). The lower-deck galley was moved up to the main floor to make room for additional baggage and freight under the floor. Although the L1011-500 could have been ready by 1977, Lockheed delayed the start because of the existing overcapacity with the airlines.

The new 50,000lb (222kN) thrust RB211-524 received its British certification at the end of 1975, the first production engine being delivered to Lockheed in March for eventual installation in Saudia's TriStar 200s. Thrust growth with refinement was expected to improve to around 53,000lb (235kN), and the engine was dimensionally the same as the earlier engines, and therefore caused no installation problems. Following flight testing in the first TriStar with the new engine fitted in both underwing and tail positions, US certification of the new engine was achieved in March 1976.

By April 1976 the overall length of the TriStar 500 was reduced to a stretch of 13ft 6in (4.1m), with an 8ft 4in (2.5m) extension ahead of the wing and 5ft 2in (1.6m) aft, to allow room for 246 passengers, reducing seat/mile costs, and resulting in the abandonment of the L1011-250 in its new production form. The British Airways version had seating for 18 first class and 217 economy passengers. The maximum take-off weight had been increased to 496,000lb (225,000kg) of which 400lb (182kg) was used in structural and undercarriage strengthening, and 54,000lb (24,516kg) more fuel was housed in the wing centre-section giving a range of 5,300 miles

BELOW: In December 1974 Gulf Air placed an order for two TriStar 200 extended-range aircraft. Here A40-TW is seen at Cambridge after maintenance by Marshall Aerospace; it has since been converted to a -200F freighter for Arrow Air as N307GB. The -200 was powered by RB211-524. *Marshall Aerospace*

ABOVE: In January 1979 British Airways placed its first order for TriStar 200s for its longer-range routes, releasing the TriStar 1s back to the European Division. TriStar 200 G-BGBC *The Shot Silk Rose* is seen in the earlier British Airways colours at Heathrow in July 1987. *Philip Birtles*

(8,500km) with a full load of passengers. This made the aircraft suitable for flights such as London-Los Angeles, New York-Buenos Aires and Sydney-Hong Kong.

Lockheed continued to study further developments, and in the autumn of 1976 was looking at a **TriStar 300** with 410 passengers on the main deck, and a further 45 in the lower deck cabin. Whenever passengers were accommodated in a lower deck cabin, a protective skid was fitted under the fuselage in the event of a forced landing with the undercarriage retracted, and although there was an access door, there were no cabin windows. This high capacity version was targeted at ANA, but was dropped when the airline ordered specially adapted Boeing 747s for its high density routes, despite the short range requirement.

By the mid-1970s the tendency was to increase the efficiency of the existing models and, with the new technology available, Lockheed began to study reduced energy capabilities, including active controls, extended wingtips and further improved RB211 engines. Should the finances allow, and if there was a market requirement later, more advanced versions could have a new high-technology wing. More straightforward developments could have the short -500 fuselage with the L1011-1 wing and de-rated engines giving short to medium range versions.

This theme was progressed further in early 1977 when Lockheed announced a range of new technology projects based on the TriStar aimed at the medium capacity short to medium range routes. The new technology included further noise reduction and fuel economy, with improved aerodynamics, active controls and some use of composites in non-load-bearing structures to reduce weight and maintenance. The **L1011-400** would have a take-off weight of between 350,500lb and 374,500lb (159,000–170,000kg), seating between 200 and 250 passengers

depending on the fuselage length. The original RB211-22 engines would be de-rated by 10 percent giving an improved overhaul and economy and a US transcontinental range of 2,700nm (5,000km). The **L1011-600** was a twin-engined version of the -400 powered by a pair of RB211-524s mounted in the existing wing positions, carrying between 174 and 200 passengers over ranges of between 2,000 and 2,700nm (3,700–5,000km) at a maximum take-off weight of 297,000lb (135,000kg).

Coming back to the more practical developments, the TriStar 200 for Saudia gained FAA certification with lower noise levels in May 1977, and by later in the year active ailerons fitted to the company-owned prototype were giving encouraging results. This was further improved by fitting extended wingtips which increased aspect ratio and lowered induced drag, cutting fuel burn by about 3.5 percent. The active ailerons relieved structural loads on the wings caused by gusts by moving the controls automatically to counter them, and these modifications were incorporated during manufacture in all but the early TriStar 500s for BA.

The idea of a **TriStar freighter** started in October 1978 with the possibility of new build aircraft for Flying Tiger Line based on the L1011-500 airframe with the windows deleted and a cargo door fitted. Maximum payload of 146,400lb (66,500kg) could be carried as far as 925nm (1,700km), but if it were reduced to 128,400lb (58,300kg) then the range increased to 3,300nm (6,100km). By September 1980 these plans had been shelved, although further studies were undertaken later based on the conversion of used aircraft, a programme eventually handled very successfully by Marshall Aerospace at Cambridge.

Development proposals then focused on an advanced technology, **Stretched TriStar 500** which would have had the longer fuselage of the TriStar 200, with strengthened wings and active controls, the range being transatlantic or transcontinental USA. A 'hot and high' TriStar 500 was proposed in the spring of 1981 powered by uprated RB211-524D4 engines developing

ABOVE: TriStar 500 D-AERL first flew in October 1980 and entered service on LTU's long-range charters. The L1011-500 had the improved RB211-524 engines, greater fuel capacity to allow increased range and higher maximum take-off weight. *Philip Birtles*

LEFT: TriStar 500 N3140D was delivered July 1982. BWIA's aircraft are in the process of being retired during 1997 and replaced by A340s. *Leo Marriott*

53,000lb (235kN) thrust. Lockheed also investigated composite ailerons and fin, the weight reduction being 65lb (30kg) over the metal equivalent on the ailerons. The composite fin saved 630lb (286kg), a 27 percent reduction, and was the largest composite structure up to that time, although it was not flown on the aircraft.

With the stopping of TriStar production, all major development ceased, but Lockheed continued to offer modest improvements to existing operators mainly aimed at better maintainability, improved reliability, greater fuel economy and extended range. As part of this process, Lockheed and Rolls-Royce offered an increased range capability in October 1985. This included re-engining with RB211-524B4s and structural strengthening to extend the range from 2,700nm to 4,500nm (5,000–8,300km). All the TriStars from No 52 onwards, apart from the L1011-500 which already had incorporated many of these improvements, were able to benefit from this series of modifications, which included strengthening in key areas of the wing, fuselage and undercarriage, increasing the maximum take-off weight by 15 percent to 496,000lb (225,000kg). Fuel capacity was increased from 150,600lb (68,400kg) to 214,000lb (97,000kg). These conversions were sold as a kit of parts for the airlines to undertake their own embodiment over a period of

five and eight weeks, and cost around $35 million per aircraft including the change of engines. The first customer for this conversion, known as the **L1011-250**, was Delta which ordered six conversion kits. In 1990 the **TriStar 150** conversion was offered to give the L1011-1 a range increase of 700nm (1,300km) to 3,100nm (5,800km); the maximum take-off weight increased by 18,000kg (40,000kg) to 470,000lb (213,000kg). Unlike the -250, these proposals did not include any changes to the engines, but gave the opportunity for improvements to about 50 L1011-1s. The **L1011-50** was a more modest conversion, increasing the gross weight to 450,000lb (204,000kg).

From 1990 onwards the major interest by Lockheed was in **cargo conversions** with up to three operators expressing interest in converting their TriStars. One L1011-1 was converted by Pemco for possible use in New Zealand, but appears to have been over-weight and was put into store in the Arizona desert. The problem arose because the TriStar's floor beams are more critically loaded than on smaller airliners. When strengthening them, great care has to be taken not to add too much weight to the structure. Lockheed had enquiries from at least two operators, who planned to phase their TriStars out of passenger service and were considering having them converted to freighters. Lockheed planned to make up to 20 such conversions at its modification centres in Ontario and Tucson. In early 1991 Saudia was considering converting up to 19 TriStars to freighters.

In mid-1992 Lockheed launched its own cargo version, known as the **Lockheed 2000**, based on the longer fuselage TriStars, despite the work already done by Marshall with the RAF conversions, because Lockheed felt that the Marshall design was not easily adaptable to civil standards. The Lockheed proposal featured a 'Mega Door' 14ft 1in by 9ft 6in (4.3 by 2.9m) for carrying oversize cargoes over ranges of 2,500nm (4,600km) with payloads weighing up to 122,200lb (55,400kg) — as compared to the Marshall 8ft 6in by 11ft 6in (2.6 by 3.5m) door, and a payload capability of up to 146,600lb (66,500kg). Design take-off weight was targeted at 466,000lb (212,000kg) with a zero fuel weight of 314,500lb (143,000kg). The modifications were to be undertaken by Lockheed Aircraft Service (LAS) at Tucson with Lockheed Aeronautical Systems (LASC) of Marietta providing the technical back-up. LAS teamed up with Avtec of Switzerland to market the conversions. Marshall Aerospace, however, continued to market its own competing design.

With the obvious proven success of the Marshall conversion programme and the difficulties experienced by Pemco, the LAS proposals were eventually dropped and the co-operation between Marshall and LASC became the sole TriStar cargo conversion programme.

Emergency systems

The flight control systems for the TriStar were fully triplicated to allow for the unlikely failure of one system, leaving two to continue the safe operation of the aircraft. The various hydraulic and electrical systems had to be widely separated in the aircraft, to avoid a catastrophic failure in one area, causing the remaining systems to be affected. The triplicated automatic flight system gave adequate redundancy in the event of a failure, and its consistent mode of operation provides predictable performance, particularly on the approach to busy airports, as well as allowing take-off and landings in poor visibility. The automatic flight system also has a number of built-in warnings to ensure that the stall is not approached, that the undercarriage is

down for landing, and a number of other areas where the edge of the flight envelope is being approached.

The new large fan engines are extremely reliable, but with three engines installed in the TriStar, it is fully capable of flying safely on two engines. No single engine failure must be allowed to interrupt any of the power generation for the safe operation of the aircraft systems, and in an emergency, the APU may be run in flight, to provide additional power. To assist the braking of the aircraft on the ground, the two wing mounted engines feature thrust reversers. This reduces brake wear, and also keeps them relatively cool, to facilitate a quick turn-round. In the event of a cabin pressurisation failure, drop down oxygen masks are available for the passengers and crew while the pilots descent to a lower altitude.

ABOVE RIGHT: Gulf Air TriStar G-BDCW was reregistered A40-TW when uprated to Srs 200 standard in 1976. Note the deployment of the thrust reversers on landing. *Lockheed*

RIGHT: Emergency evacuation slide positions and test details. *Lockheed*

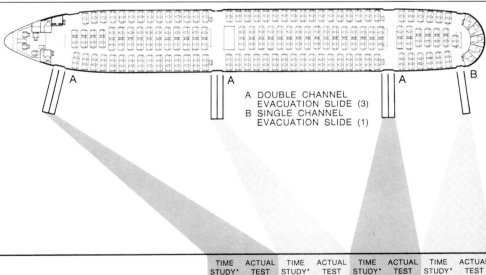

A DOUBLE CHANNEL EVACUATION SLIDE (3)
B SINGLE CHANNEL EVACUATION SLIDE (1)

		TIME STUDY*	ACTUAL TEST	TIME STUDY*	ACTUAL TEST	TIME STUDY*	ACTUAL TEST	TIME STUDY*	ACTUAL TEST
	CREW POSITIONING / AND EXIT OPEN (SECONDS)	10	3	10	4	10	3	10	3
	SLIDE DEPLOYED (SECONDS)	10	6	10	8	10	5	10	6
20/80 MIXED CLASS 256 PASSENGERS 15 CREW	NUMBER OF EVACUEES	78	NOT DEMONSTRATED	78	NOT DEMONSTRATED	78	NOT DEMONSTRATED	37	NOT DEMONSTRATED
	EVACUATION TIME (SECONDS)	49.14		49.14		49.14		49.21	
	TOTAL TIME (SECONDS)	69.14		69.14		69.14		69.21	
ALL ECONOMY 345 PASSENGERS 15/10** CREW	NUMBER OF EVACUEES	104	103	104	99	104	100	48	53
	EVACUATION TIME (SECONDS)	65.52	66	65.52	70	65.52	65	63.84	65
	TOTAL TIME (SECONDS)	85.52	75	85.52	82	85.52	73	83.84	74

*STUDY EVACUATION RATE BASED ON AVERAGE 1.26 SECONDS PER PASSENGER FOR TYPE A EXIT AND 1.33 SECONDS FOR TYPE I EXIT
**15 CREW ASSUMED IN STUDY ESTIMATE, 10 IN DEMONSTRATION

5 IN SERVICE

ORDERS

The launch orders and options were from Eastern and TWA — 50 for Eastern and 44 from TWA. Although sufficient to give an initial confidence in launching the aircraft into development, they were, of course, insufficient to justify the programme without substantial further sales. During the design and development programme, Lockheed was able to generate sufficient sales' prospects to make it worth proceeding, despite all the financial difficulties. Eventually Eastern Airlines put a total of 31 TriStars into service operating mainly from their Miami base, but also sharing with Delta some of the facilities at Atlanta. TWA put 35 aircraft into service on world-wide and continental US routes. As an offset for the choice of a British rather than US-manufactured engine, Air Holdings ordered 30 TriStars, with options on a further 20, for sale outside the USA.

The Eastern Airlines' order was worth $860 million (£358 million) with the first batch of aircraft to be delivered during 1972, and the remaining 25 options were planned over the next two years. In fact Eastern received its first 10 TriStars before deliveries began to TWA. These started with a batch of six aircraft, although the first production TriStar was painted for a while in TWA colours before being allocated to Eastern. The TWA order was worth $750 million (£313 million) and deliveries were scheduled along a similar timetable to Eastern's. The Air Holdings' firm order was worth $442 million (£184 million) with deliveries available from late 1973 when sufficient capacity became available on the production line. Including the options, the Air Holdings contract was worth $720 million (£300 million).

TOP: TWA and Eastern were the launch customers for the TriStar, TWA ordering 44. Here a prototype TriStar is seen on test in the early TWA livery. *Lockheed*

ABOVE: N31033 was delivered to TWA in February 1976 and is seen in the airline's later livery. *Lockheed*

LEFT: Orders and options from Eastern were for up to 50 Tristars with deliveries commencing in 1972. Amongst the last three aircraft delivered to Eastern in November 1976 was L1011-1 N334EA, seen here carrying the fleet name 'Whisperliner'. The photograph was taken at Toronto in March 1984; this aircraft was acquired by Delta in September 1991 and is currently stored. *Philip Birtles*

Top: The second customer for the new long-range TriStar 500 was Delta, which ordered an initial two in January 1978, with options on three more. Transatlantic services were started in the interim on 1 May 1978 with two L1011-200s leased from TWA, pending delivery of the new aircraft. Here is Delta's N728DA, a TriStar 1 which was delivered in November 1979. *Lockheed*

Above: Delta TriStar 500 N767DA was originally delivered to Air Canada as C-GAGI making its last service on 27 October 1991. The aircraft is seen about to depart from London Gatwick in May 1993 and is still in service with the airline. *Philip Birtles*

Right: PSA TriStar 1 N10114 seen at Farnborough in 1974. *Philip Birtles*

Early major new customers were Delta, today the largest operator of the TriStar, and Northeast. The Delta contract was for a total of 24 aircraft worth $360 million (£150 million) with the first 12 due for delivery in 1972, and the remainder the following year. The Northeast order was for four aircraft plus four options worth $50 million (£25 million), deliveries to be during 1972. Orders within one month of the launch decision therefore totalled 152 aircraft worth $2,500 million (£1,035 million) of which Rolls-Royce would receive $385 million (£160 million). Northeast placed two more firm orders in mid-1968, with plans to introduce the TriStars on its Boston–Florida and New York–Florida routes, eventually expanding to link Montreal, Baltimore, Philadelphia and Washington with the Florida destinations, particularly during the cold northern winters when people like to escape to the warmer south. The Northeast TriStars were configured with 40 first class and 227 tourist class seats.

Despite the temporary downturn in the economy which

reduced demand for seats, the airlines were keen to introduce the advanced technology TriStar, with its comfortable and roomy wide-bodied cabin. Its seat-mile costs were significantly lower than any of the earlier generation jet airliners, giving it the range flexibility of flying economically from the US coast-to-coast, or the shorter high density commuter routes such as Phoenix or San Francisco to Los Angeles. The TriStar was also compatible with the Boeing 747 as far as terminal facilities and cargo containers were concerned, and had a similar spacious cabin.

The Air Holdings contract covered all export sales from the US, leaving Lockheed the exclusive rights within the US. As part of the Air Holdings agreement, they would provide all the sales support including the customer financing needs through Lazard Brothers, the City of London merchant bankers. Lockheed expected overseas sales to reach 175 TriStars by 1975, with predictions of the overall export market being up to 500 aircraft by 1980. In December 1968 Air Holdings made its first sale: 10 TriStars to Air Canada with options on nine more, although the options were later used for five of the developed TriStar 500s. Air Jamaica had placed an order direct with Lockheed for two TriStars in April 1968 worth $30 million (£12.5 million), but this was taken out of the Air Holdings' allocation. If Air Holdings had not sold any TriStars, the total potential liability was estimated to be £15 million, but the company was protected by an indemnity from Rolls-Royce and the British Government guaranteed half the commitment up to a maximum of £50 million. Additional orders in December were from the finance companies Air Finance and Turner & Haas for three and two aircraft respectively, for lease to operators. The British liability was reduced to £10 million, and both Rolls-Royce and the British Government received an appropriate share of the proceeds.

In early 1970 Northeast Airlines began to hold merger talks with Northwest, and as the latter airline had already placed substantial orders for the DC-10, it resulted in the TriStars for Northeast being cancelled. Northeast eventually merged with Delta on 1 April 1972.

The first TriStar rolled out on 1 September 1970, a day that also saw the announcement of an order from Pacific Southwest Airlines (PSA) who issued a letter of intent for two TriStars with reservations on a further three delivery positions. At the time PSA was the largest intrastate airline and the first two aircraft were to be allocated to the busy 284nm (526km) Los Angeles–San Francisco route, starting in 1972, with the other three aircraft following the next year. The TriStars were expected to cope with the anticipated growth of the route over the next five or six years, but the airline was experiencing some overcapacity at the time, making the order conditional upon satisfactory finance. Both the aircraft and engines were seen as particularly suitable for the relatively short sectors which were typical of the PSA operations. These TriStars were painted in a bright red and orange colour scheme with a black smile under the nose.

In September 1971 Air Holdings was taken over fully by British & Commonwealth Shipping (B&C), which had previously held 46 percent of the shares. B&C therefore assumed responsibility for non-American TriStar sales at a time when the US and British governments, Rolls-Royce and Lockheed were in negotiation over the future of the aircraft. All Nippon placed options for six TriStars in March 1971, but no money changed hands because of the uncertainty of the programme.

Towards the end of October 1971 Lockheed clarified the order situation with the TriStar: There were 103 firm orders with 46 options, which had been confirmed by non-returnable deposits paid by the airlines. However B&C had inherited the Air Holdings agreement, and under the terms of the contract they had failed to meet the 1 October deadline for the progress payments on the 29 unsold aircraft. B&C was still expected to take the aircraft as the share of RB211 economic offsets, but the terms of the contract stipulated that if the key progress payment was missed, Lockheed would have the right to waive the contract and retain all the money deposited until 31 July 1977 to help finance the ongoing production programme. As each of the remaining 29 aircraft were sold, refunds would be made to B&C, with all outstanding funds being returned by July 1977. The Air Jamaica order was later cancelled, but the deposits made by Air Canada were refunded to B&C as Air Canada made its own progress payments to Lockheed. Lockheed therefore took over responsibility for the world-wide sales of the TriStar with B&C as a marketing partner.

Within a short time of this agreement being confirmed, the first British order for TriStars was announced. It was worth £19 million by the Luton-based holiday charter operator Court Line and was for two aircraft plus three options. Airlease was the actual purchaser of the aircraft, which would then be leased to Court Line. The first two aircraft were due for delivery in time for the 1973 summer season, with the second buys due one per year from 1974 onwards. Court Line was the first European company to order TriStars, and the first charter operator to put a wide-bodied airliner into service. The TriStars were to be allo-

BELOW: Pacific Southwest Airlines' N10114 at Farnborough in 1974. Delivered in 1974, N10114 was converted to Srs 100 in 1979 and sold to Aero Peru. It became C-GIFE of Worldways Canada in 1985. *Philip Birtles*

ABOVE: The first Court Line TriStar at the airline's Luton base shortly after delivery. *Philip Birtles*

cated to Clarkson Holidays tours, which had just signed a five-year contract with Court Line and required a high density and high utilisation operation. The TriStar, with its 2,700-mile range, would bring all the major holiday destinations in Europe, north Africa and the eastern Mediterranean within non-stop range of Britain, with the possibility of increasing winter utilisation. Typically, for the competitive cost, the TriStars were configured to carry 400 passengers in a one class 3-4-3 seat layout. To speed passenger entry and exit, double-width doors were installed; to make ground handling easier at the more remote destinations, the aircraft was fitted with integral airstairs located in the cargo holds and baggage handling systems — because Court Line was not concerned with carrying cargo like the major scheduled carriers, the space taken by these systems was not critical. Distinctive features of the Court Line fleet were the colour schemes, the first TriStar being painted in an overall orange livery and the second in pink. The contract was finally signed on 12 August 1972, with the airline's first TriStar making its maiden flight in late January 1973.

Towards the end of 1972 there were problems with the PSA contract which was being renegotiated following the Lockheed crisis. PSA decided to re-evaluate the TriStar against the competition, even though small deposits had already been paid. However, the choice of the TriStar was confirmed in September 1972 by the ordering of five aircraft. The first was due for delivery in spring 1974 and featured a lower deck cocktail lounge. Because the high density Californian operations required quick turnarounds, the PSA TriStars were fitted with four extra-wide doors; on top of this, 100 passengers with carry on baggage were allowed to board through a lower deck auxiliary entrance into the passenger lounge. The first PSA TriStar was delivered to the airline on 2 July 1974.

Entry into Service

The first airline delivery was TriStar N306EA to Eastern on 6 April 1972. The first service was from Miami to New York on 26 April with 123 passengers, as a substitute for a DC-8. Three Eastern captains had already been qualified on the aircraft, thus allowing the first commercial service to be flown before the new aircraft was delivered in sufficient numbers to allow it to operate on full schedules.

TWA received its first TriStar in early May and on Sunday 25 June 1972 TriStar N31001 departed St Louis on the inaugural flight to Los Angeles carrying a full complement of 30 first class passengers; only 10 seats out of 176 were unoccupied in the economy class. Take-off weight was 378,000lb (172,000kg) including 87,000lb (39,500kg) of fuel for the 1,527-mile (2,457km) flight. The operation of the aircraft was under automatic control from lining up on the runway at St Louis to the roll-out at Los Angeles, a remarkable achievement for a new aircraft at the start of its operational career. The aircraft cruised at Mach 0.87 at 31,000ft (9,500m) giving a true airspeed of 520kts (598mph/962kph) and a flight time of 3hr 10min.

In the middle of 1972, following successful negotiations with Lockheed, Delta confirmed its order for the TriStar; it would later become the largest — and a very enthusiastic — operator of the type. The DC-10s on order as an insurance were transferred to United and leased back temporarily to Delta, while deliveries of the TriStars were established.

The battle for new sales continued aggressively between Lockheed and Douglas Aircraft: as part of a major world tour for both aircraft, Japan — where there was a need for a number of aircraft of their capacity — was singled out for attention in July 1972. On 23 July TriStar N305EA flew to Osaka, while the DC-10 visited Tokyo, ready for demonstration flights the following day over the busy Japanese trunk route, changing places as they did so.

On completion of the Asian part of the tour, the TriStar returned to Palmdale for the preparations for a European visit finishing at the Farnborough Air Show in September. The aircraft was in the basic Eastern colours with the potential customer logos added as appropriate; BEA was the one for Britain, British Government approval having been announced for the TriStar order on 7 August. The BEA preference for the TriStar was no secret and the initial order was for six standard TriStars with options on six extended-range versions. Deliveries were to start late 1974 for services to start in early 1975. With the merger of BEA and BOAC into British Airways (BA) imminent (they would formally merge on 1 April 1974), the contract was strictly

LEFT: TriStar 1 N305EA at the 1972 Farnborough Air Show was borrowed from Eastern for the event and painted in BEA colours. *Philip Birtles*

Philadelphia to Los Angeles with a stop at Chicago, also linking Chicago with San Francisco and Phoenix. In the following month, the FAA approved the operation of the TWA TriStars in Cat 3a weather conditions, the first time this approval was granted. To achieve this the TriStar had quadrupled redundancy of the major appropriate systems, and the automatic operation included the closing of the throttle, operation of the spoilers and steering on the runway until the turn off.

a BEA one, and required the approval of the BA board as part of the integration of the operations of the two airlines. The order for the aircraft was worth £20 million, and a further £20 million was allocated to all the support services required by the introduction of the new airliner. BEA could see a need for up to 18 TriStars on its network alone by 1980, while the old BOAC routes could effectively use a number of the extended-range versions. It was also expected that Airtours, the holiday charter subsidiary of the national airline, could also use some TriStar capacity.

During the overseas demonstrations the aircraft flew 91,000 miles (146,000km) in 138 flights, logging 198 flying hours. Departure rate was a creditable 99 percent with 8,500 passengers carried from 35 airports, often achieving three sorties per day. By August 1972 16 TriStars had flown, with the 21st aircraft — the first for Air Canada — in final assembly, and a total of 22 scheduled for delivery by the end of the year. Air Canada was planning to introduce the aircraft on 15 February 1973 with a 256-passenger mixed-class layout.

When BEA signed the contract for six TriStars on 26 September 1972 the options were increased to 12 further aircraft. It was felt that, in the typical European weather environment, the automatic landing facility, which BEA had pioneered with the Trident a decade earlier, would bring economic and operational gains. In addition the quiet engine operation would avoid some of the night curfews experienced by the operators of the noisier airliners.

TWA expanded its TriStar operations in September 1972 by putting the aircraft on daily transcontinental routes from

The success of the Japanese demonstrations was confirmed for Lockheed when All-Nippon Airways (ANA) placed an initial order for six TriStars in October with deliveries due in November 1973; ANA would later add options on a further 15 aircraft. ANA was the sixth largest domestic airline in the world, with the operation of the Tokyo–Osaka route probably the second most dense anywhere. Over the previous five years the airline had experienced a high passenger/kilometre growth rate of between 35 and 45 percent. This made it the largest Japanese domestic airline, with 59 routes served in 1971, making 420 round trips and offering 28,000 seats daily. In 1970 ANA had carried 7.61 million passengers and flew 2,870 million passenger miles (4,629 million km), the average stage length being around 372 miles (600km) – all of them domestic.

In the same month the Düsseldorf-based charter airline LTU signed a letter of intent for two TriStars, with deliveries due in May 1973 and the spring of 1975. They were to be used on daily tourist flights to the Mediterranean resorts and Canary Islands with seating for up to 330 passengers in an all-economy layout. Delta also increased its options by six, bringing its total commitment to 18 firm orders plus 12 options. At this stage there were firm commitments for 184 aircraft from 11 airlines.

By the end of the first six months of operation both

BELOW: British Airtours TriStar 100 G-BBAJ seen at London Gatwick on 5 February 1986. Previously delivered to BA who flew the last service on 28 October 1989, this aircraft is now in operation with British Caledonian. *Nick Granger*

ABOVE: British Airways placed the launch order for the long-range TriStar 500 in August 1976 by converting six of its earlier options. The first two aircraft were used for the certification of the new variant, the third aircraft being the first delivery to the airline on 30 April 1979. The fourth TriStar 500 for BA was G-BFCD, which was displayed at the Farnborough Air Show in September 1980, having been delivered to the airline in May 1979. It is now in service as ZD951 with No 216 Squadron as a tanker/passenger transport K Mk 1, based at Brize Norton. *Rolls-Royce*

Eastern and TWA had six TriStars in service and the RB211 engines had been working well, with the predicted removal rate of 1.1 per 1,000 hours slightly bettered, although due to the modular nature of the engine it was probably more appropriate to quote the in-flight shut-down rate of 0.55 per 1,000 hours. Eastern commenced operations on an average daily utilisation of eight hours with 2.8 hours as an average flight duration. TWA had started at a daily 10-hour utilisation with 3.5 hours as the average stage length. These operations gave the aircraft, engines and equipment ample opportunity to sort out any teething problems, but reliability was very good. As each of the two airlines had differing peak seasons, TWA and Eastern operated a reciprocal leasing programme to spread the capacity more evenly.

Returning to the more mundane tasks of producing TriStars, the first aircraft for Air Canada was rolled out at Palmdale in late December 1972, for delivery the following month. Initial services were planned to start in mid-February on the Toronto–Miami route, taking the cold Canadians to the warm Florida south. In March the aircraft were also put on the busy Montreal–Toronto–Vancouver transcontinental trunk route. In addition to its 10 firm orders, Air Canada had a joint arrangement with Eastern and the Haas-Turner finance lease organisation to share two TriStars at times to suit peak traffic demands. Air Canada estimated its total need for TriStars to be some 30 aircraft, including some long-range developments.

The first British-registered TriStar, Court Line's G-BAAA, named *Halcyon Days*, was delivered to Luton on 5 March 1973, ready for its first service to Palma on 2 April. An annual utilisation of 3,000 hours was planned for each of the TriStars. The initial crew training of the first five or six crews was completed in Palmdale, the remainder being trained at Luton, where the airline's own Redifon flight simulator was installed. The introduction of the TriStars was welcome at Luton airport and the destinations, because of the much quieter operation. Each TriStar could carry the equivalent of three and a half of the noisier BAC One-Eleven loads, and they were allowed their full allocation of 340 night movements. Although the TriStar economics were comparable with the BAC One-Eleven on the shorter routes, it was increasingly competitive over the longer ranges. It was also planned to use the TriStars on flights to the Caribbean, where Clarksons had hotel interests, with a technical stop at the Azores. Because of financial problems with Clarksons Holidays, the parent company, Shipping Industrial Holdings, sold a controlling 85 percent interest of its holiday tour subsidiary to Court Line for a nominal sum, some 40 percent of the Court Line business being generated by Clarksons' five-year contract. Due to the more difficult financial situation Court Line was considering deferring its third TriStar option and delaying or cancelling the options on the further two aircraft. Meanwhile its second TriStar, *Halcyon Breeze*, was delivered to Luton on 3 May 1973, flying the longest non-stop flight to date — the 5,500-mile (8,900km) great circle route direct from Palmdale — fully automatically from take-off to touch-down.

In the first year of commercial operations, the TriStar fleet, consisting of 25 aircraft, had flown nearly 30,000 hours and carried over 1.3 million passengers on more than 11,000 revenue earning flights.

The first TriStar was delivered to LTU at Düsseldorf on 29 May 1973, and on 7 September the first Delta TriStar was rolled off the production line for delivery to the airline on 3 October. Services commenced in December covering mainly the eastern destinations in the US — New York, Philadelphia, Atlanta, Miami, Tampa and New Orleans — as well as flying west to Houston. Meanwhile the order book continued to grow, with ANA confirming eight of its TriStar options in September, with two more in October. This brought its total firm requirements to 16 TriStars for use not only on its domestic network, but to branch out on some overseas charter flights to Manila from Tokyo. Also in October the European Division of British Airways increased its firm orders to nine TriStars with a further nine still on option.

Effects of the fuel crisis

The fuel crisis which started late in 1973 brought further financial problems to Lockheed and the airlines. Eastern Airlines was forced to defer nine TriStars because of overcapacity, leading to an expensive slow down in the production line. At the end of 1973 Lockheed had orders for 199 TriStars with 56 delivered, but as the slow down restricted the vital long-range developments of the aircraft, exploratory merger talks were being held separately with Hughes and Textron. The cash position improved when Delta, TWA and ANA requested early deliveries of a total of seven aircraft, as the more fuel efficient and larger capacity TriStars could score over the aircraft they were replacing, especially as fuel was in some cases being rationed to 90 percent of the previous year's levels.

In March 1974 Cathay Pacific signed a letter of intent for two TriStars and two options with an extended-range capability simply achieved by putting additional fuel in a wing centre-section tank, increasing the take-off weight to 460,000lb (209,000kg). The Saudia order later the same month was for two L1011-100s with options on three more; the additional range was achieved by carrying more fuel in the wings, but without the centre-section tanks. The take-off weight of the Saudia aircraft was increased to 450,000lb (204,000kg); range was 4,000 miles (6,400km) with up to 259 passengers.

After only one season of operation, one of the early casualties of the fuel crisis was Court Line who had to borrow heavily in early 1974; in June a dramatic drop in their share values led to trading being suspended on the London Stock Exchange. The difficulties had a number of causes — mainly the reduction by one third of holiday booking in 1974, com-

bined with a depression in the tanker operating part of the business, losses in the shipbuilding work and in Caribbean investments. The British Government was involved in a rescue package, making £15 million available in return for the nationalisation of the shipbuilding parts of the business. However this only put off the final collapse: Court Line announced on 15 August that it was going into liquidation, stranding nearly 50,000 holidaymakers overseas. Fortunately a £3.3 million bond had been deposited with the Association of British Travel Agents (ABTA), allowing a number of other British airlines to mount a recovery operation. The Court Line fleet was grounded, the TriStars being stored at Luton, until flown back to Palmdale for refurbishment and sale to Cathay Pacific in the autumn of 1977.

The first TriStar for BA, G-BBAE, made its first flight from Palmdale on 3 September 1974 and was delivered to London Heathrow on 21 October with 20 first class and 300 economy seats. In November BA placed an order for further standard TriStars bringing its total to 15 aircraft. During late December and January 1975, BA carried out a series of route proving flights with the first three TriStars to be delivered. The first commercial service was from London to Paris on 12 January, followed by Brussels and Madrid the next day. Malaga and Palma were soon added, and when the fleet had grown to five TriStars by the end of February, they were phased into the services to Amsterdam, Tel Aviv, Faro, Alicante and Athens ready to meet the full summer schedules on 1 April.

ANA signed an agreement for a further seven TriStars in September 1974, conditional upon the Japanese Government allowing wide-bodied jet airliners to operate from Osaka, but even without this approval two TriStars would be needed. Saudia placed the first order for two of what was a longer range version of the standard TriStar, the L1011-200, on 19 September 1974. The -200 was powered by the uprated RB211-524 engines developing 48,000lb (213kN) of thrust, a 6,000lb (27kN) improvement over the earlier engines. ANA's earlier two aircraft were to be modified to the same standard

BELOW: Saudia operates the last TriStar built, L1011-500 HZ-HM5 for the Saudi Arabian Government. It was originally ordered for the Algerian Government, but not delivered. It is seen here at Cambridge Airport after servicing by Marshall Aerospace. *Marshall Aerospace*

giving a transatlantic range of 4,700 miles (7,600km). In November 1974 Delta had replaced its DC-10s with TriStars and converted three of its options to firm orders, bringing its total orders to 21 aircraft. In December Gulf Air ordered four extended TriStar -100s with four options, delivery to start in January 1976. With the take-off weight increased to 466,000lb (212,000kg), 18,000lb (8,200kg) of additional fuel could be carried in the wing centre-section, and although the aircraft were initially fitted with RB211-22B engines, more powerful versions could be fitted later if required.

The continuing fuel crisis in 1975 and the resulting recession in the air transport industry, particularly in the US, meant that Eastern and TWA had excess capacity of about four TriStars each, and PSA had to ground its two, replacing them temporarily with Boeing 727s until the position improved; they were reintroduced in June. LTU bought a TriStar from Eastern in July and Saudia's first extended L1011-100 was delivered in July with services starting on 15 August. In January 1976 Delta ordered one more TriStar, the first sale for over a year, but Cathay cancelled two of its options, and Saudia took two new TWA aircraft straight off the production line. Gulf Air's first TriStar was delivered at the end of January 1976 with regular services of these plush furnished aircraft starting between London and the Gulf on 1 April.

In April 1976 firm TriStar orders stood at 157 aircraft with another 50 options covering the standard L1011-1, the extended range L1011-100 and the longer range L1011-200. A total of 127 had been delivered, but the 1976 production rate was expected to be down to between nine and twelve aircraft, because of the continuing fuel crisis. This also made Lockheed's finances more difficult, especially with the costs of developing the improved versions, and the slow down in production. Eight of the remaining 30 aircraft were for BA, which required them to be delivered gradually up to 1982. The rival DC-10 was also lacking sales, but more had been sold overall, while Airbus was continuing to obtain orders. New orders were also depressed by the number of second-hand TriStars available. The first two PSA TriStars were grounded again and the other three remained undelivered and the two ex-Court Line

aircraft were stored at Palmdale. Eastern had disposed of three of its fleet and was keen to dispose of more, and TWA was selling production line places to other operators.

Despite the problems of overcapacity with many of the world's airline routes, the Gulf region showed rapid growth, and BA put a couple of the European Division's TriStar 1s on the Middle East routes gaining 45 percent of the market. This buoyancy was confirmed further when Saudia broke the 18-month lull in sales by ordering three more RB211-524 powered L1011-200s for deliveries starting in September 1977, two of the ex-TWA allocations being re-engined on the production line.

Air Canada planned to start transatlantic services with its TriStar 1s, and therefore decided to modify them to -100 standard, making available the centre-section tank capacity of 19,000lb (8,600kg) of fuel and increasing the take-off weight by 36,000lb (16,300kg) to 466,000lb (212,000kg) for a modest increase in empty weight of 1,400lb (640kg). This extended the range with 257 passengers by 900 miles (1,700km) to 3,700nm (6,800km) and transatlantic operations started in April 1977 on routes from Montreal and Toronto to London, Frankfurt and Paris. In late 1977 TWA also converted four of its TriStar 1s to the L1011-100 configuration with more planned to follow, allowing them to start transatlantic flights in the spring of 1978.

In the middle of 1976 the first indications of the move out of the world depression were becoming apparent with some signs of growth in passenger numbers. In August Delta confirmed two of its options for delivery in May and December 1978. In October 1976 LTU came to an agreement with Lockheed to return its two TriStar 1s and replace them with the three undelivered PSA aircraft. This gave LTU a high density layout and a consistent standard of aircraft, avoiding having a mixed fleet of the two early TriStars and a new one to a different standard. The first of the new aircraft was delivered in mid-March 1977 and LTU became the first regular transatlantic TriStar operator on 4 April with advanced booking charter flights between Düsseldorf and New York. Using the lower deck passenger lounge as specified by PSA, with its own entry door and air-stairs, provided seating overall for 330 passengers.

Delta confirmed a further option in February 1977 with five options still remaining, bringing the total Delta fleet to 25 TriStars by the end of 1978. They ordered two more in August

BELOW: Gulf Air A40-TT a -200 series aircraft – was delivered in December 1981. *Leo Marriott*

ABOVE: Ex-Eastern TriStar 1 N323EA acquired by LTU, then delivered to Cathay Pacific. This aircraft was eventually bought by Air Atlanta and used for spares' recovery in January 1997 at Bruntingthorpe. *Nick Granger*

977 and in October 1978, Delta confirmed orders for five more TriStar 1s, with a further 15 options, taking deliveries out to 1984. ANA increased its fleet to 20 TriStars when it placed an order for three more in April 1977. Saudia increased its fleet of TriStars to 10 by ordering two L1011-200s in May 1977, followed by three more in May 1978. Saudia's first L1011-200 was delivered on 27 May 1977. In January 1979, BA ordered its first two L1011-200s, powered by RB211-524 engines, for delivery the following March, releasing the TriStar 1s back to the European Division. Gulf Air ordered a pair of L1011-200s in August 1979 to add to its four -100s and these were to be fitted with the new flight management system (FMS) as offered on the later L1011-500. BA increased its total orders for TriStars to 23 in September 1979 with a contract for six more L1011-200s and with deliveries to commence six months later.

At this stage Lockheed was claiming total sales of 270 TriStars with a further 71 options, having sold 23 aircraft in the previous two months including 14 to unannounced customers. Delta continued to add to its fleet when it converted two options to firm orders for L1011-1s in March 1980 bringing its total to 32 in service, eight on order and 13 options. During 1980 Delta added three more TriStars and three more the following year. Delta planned to build its TriStar fleet up to 44 aircraft by mid-1983, with 10 scheduled for delivery over the next two years and seven options remaining. Gulf Air added a seventh TriStar in spring 1980.

THE L1011-500

Lockheed was finally able to develop a true long-range version of the TriStar, the L1011-500, which was optimised for the longer thin routes. After a highly competitive sales battle between Lockheed, Boeing and McDonnell Douglas, British Airways announced its decision in August 1976 to place a launch order for this new variant, by converting six of its options for the earlier aircraft, and adding a further six options. The BA aircraft were to be configured with 18 first class and 217 economy class seats and with delivery due in 1979, the aircraft would be ideal for the long thin routes from London to Philadelphia, the US West Coast, the Caribbean and the Gulf routes.

The initial L1011-500 marketing was to approach existing customers to determine interest in the new shorter-fuselage long-range version. As many still had in operation fleets of first-generation jet airliners, which needed replacement, Lockheed predicted sales of up to 244 TriStar 500s. Delta, always an enthusiastic TriStar operator, ordered two in January 1978 with three options, for use on its newly approved Atlanta–London Gatwick route. To start the route quickly, Delta leased from TWA a pair of TriStar 1s modified to L1011-200 standard with RB211-524 engines. Operating at a reduced payload, these aircraft started services on 1 May 1978. Delta added another firm order for a -500 in March 1979, its first being delivered six months later.

A significant new customer in April 1978 was PanAm with an order for 12 TriStar 500s, with options on a further 14, all to be powered by the RB211-524 engines, although the airline had

BELOW: TriStar 500 D-AERL made its last flight with LTU on 30 April 1996, before being acquired by Alia as JY-AGF. *Nick Granger*

wanted Pratt & Whitney engines to give commonality with its Boeing 747 fleet. The aircraft were fitted with extended wingtips and active ailerons to improve the ride and the fuel efficiency, and when they entered service in April 1980, they were used on the transatlantic and South American routes replacing Boeing 707s. In September 1978 British West Indian Airways (BWIA), another new customer, gained approval from its government to place an order for two TriStar 500s with two options, the first being delivered in January 1980. The two options were converted in September, and the airline still flies these aircraft on the long-range London Heathrow–Caribbean route.

The first TriStar 500 was rolled out at Palmdale on 12 October 1978. Type development flying used this and the second aircraft, taking over 530 flying hours. The maiden flight of 2hr 30min was on 16 October, one month ahead of schedule. The first 500 aircraft for BA was the third 500 off the production line and was delivered to the airline on 30 April 1979 allowing services to commence to Abu Dhabi in May and extensions to Singapore the following month, by which time the fleet had grown to three aircraft. The new FMS saved fuel by controlling the performance of the aircraft precisely. It held the speed to within one knot (1.15mph/1.85kph) of the selected figure, and the aircraft would rise and sink through 100ft (30m) height band. The L1011-500s were powered by RB211-524B engines giving a thrust of 50,000lb (222kN).

Another existing airline to opt for the longer-range variant was Air Canada, which ordered six TriStar 500s in April 1979 as part of its 10-year fleet renewal programme with nine options,

which were later cancelled. The 244-seat aircraft were intended for the transatlantic routes entering service in 1981, the first aircraft being delivered in February. LTU also added two all-economy 276-seat TriStar 500s to its fleet in May 1979 for delivery the following year. These were to take over from earlier versions the longer range charter flights from Europe to New York, Los Angeles, the Caribbean, Thailand and Sri Lanka. TAP Air Portugal became a new customer when it ordered three TriStar 500s in September 1979, with options on another two. Confirmation was delayed by the Portuguese Government while the airline proved an economic case for the new aircraft, as it had suffered heavy losses over the previous two years. Negotiations were then delayed further by industrial action in mid-1980, but the order was finally confirmed in October. The first of the eventual fleet of five aircraft was delivered in November 1982, and two more were leased from Alia until 1995, when they were returned to the leasing company, Partnairs.

The first PanAm TriStar 500 made its maiden flight from Palmdale on 16 November 1979 — the first of two for the airline to be used to gain FAA certification over a period of 330 flying hours. Certification was achieved on 1 April 1980, with particular reference to the extended wingtips and active flying controls. PanAm started its first scheduled service into London Gatwick in July 1980 as part of the round-the-world service.

At the end of 1979 Alia Royal Jordanian ordered five TriStar 500s with four more to follow, including one for the Jordanian Royal Flight. These TriStars were for the European and transatlantic routes and are still in operation today.

LEFT: Air Canada ordered six TriStar 500s in April 1979 for use on its long-range transatlantic services. Air Canada TriStar 500 C-GAGF is seen shortly after arrival at London Heathrow in June 1989; it was sold to Delta in August 1991 as N764DA. *Philip Birtles*

ABOVE: Royal Jordanian Airlines' JY-AGC was delivered in 1982 when the airline was called Alia. *Leo Marriott*

The final airline customer for the TriStar was AirLanka which ordered two TriStar 500s in March 1980 with options on two more, the plan being to replace the Boeing 707s on the long-haul routes to Europe. AirLanka also leased various other TriStars, and bought two from ANA in March 1981.

Although provision had not been made to retrofit the BA TriStar 500s with extended wingtips and active controls, it was decided they were necessary due to a significant short fall in fuel consumption. The wingtip extensions adding 9ft (2.75m) to the overall span, reducing the drag and giving 2.5 percent saving in fuel consumption. At the same time the more fuel efficient RB211-524B2 engines were fitted and the first modified TriStar 500 was returned to BA at the end of 1980.

Production ceases

Following the eventual confirmation of the TAP order, sales prospects for the TriStar diminished with the prospect of a few top-ups in the Delta fleet, while there were already a number of TriStars available on the second-hand market. The new-generation wide-bodied Airbus family and Boeing 767 made further sales of the TriStar increasingly unlikely and continuing losses in the production programme suggested in 1981 that production might have to be stopped. The first quarter loss on TriStar production in 1981 was $36 million (£15 million), an increase over the same period in the previous year. The order backlog was for 44 aircraft, with 18 TriStars to be produced during the year, not all of which were sold. Even after cancellation costs, by stopping TriStar production Lockheed would be significantly more profitable, and it was therefore decided that production would cease if fewer than 10 aircraft were produced in a year.

Air India was a good prospect for seven or eight TriStars with deliveries to commence in early 1983, but the order was never confirmed. Lockheed finally decided at the end of 1981 to close the TriStar production line in 1984 because of the depressed commercial airliner market, which was not expected to improve until at least 1986. To make the programme viable, Lockheed would need to have sales to support at least 24 aircraft per year from 1985 to 1990, but the competition from the later jet airliners suggested that such levels could not be sustained. With firm orders outstanding for 21 TriStars and about 40 options, Lockheed guaranteed to complete any converted options providing they were confirmed by mid-1982. Total losses on the overall TriStar programme amounted to nearly $2,500 million (£1,000 million) including $400 million written off after tax for the closure of the line. The final number built was 250 including the first aircraft which never entered service.

RECENT HISTORY

The world's TriStar fleet had a persistent high level of achievement in reliability, maintainability and as a profit maker for the operators, even if it had not been profitable for the manufacturer. However, the time had to come when it began to reach the twilight of its career.

In the spring of 1989 — 17 years after the first commercial TriStar operation — Gulf Air started the replacement process by placing an order for six extended-range Boeing 767-300ERs to take over from its 11 long-range TriStars; the first withdrawals were due in midyear. In mid-1992 it announced plans to sell its fleet of eight TriStars to help raise money towards a fleet of new wide-bodies; then, following sales of its 767s, planned to put three stored TriStars back into service for the summer 1997 season.

In 1988–89, the AirLanka operations were dominated by the TriStar fleet of four aircraft, with a fifth one to be added. Although business traffic was important, tourism was essential to the fortunes of the airline, and the continual civil unrest caused fluctuations in the tourist trade, especially following the loss of 16 lives in the TriStar sabotaged on the ground at Colombo in 1986. In 1988, the UK and other governments warned against travel to Sri Lanka causing an immediate slump in visitors to the island, but with a more settled environment in recent years, the situation has improved significantly. AirLanka also considered taking advantage of the TriStar cargo conversion, but to date no progress has been made. With the benefit

ABOVE: TriStar 200 G-BHBR on lease to Kuwait Airways at Gatwick airport on 1 June 1992; alongside is a Comet first-generation jet airliner. This TriStar flew its last service with BA on 8 November 1991, and has now been converted to a -200F freighter for American International. *Nick Granger*

LEFT: Air America TriStar 1 N301EA which was originally delivered to Eastern and later operated with Faucett as OB-1455. It was dismantled for spares' recovery at Miami in May 1994. *Nick Granger*

BELOW: Aer Lingus TriStar 100 G-BBAF seen at London Gatwick while on short-term lease from Caledonian. This aircraft was originally delivered to BA, who flew their last service on 5 November 1990, before passing it to Caledonian. *Nick Granger*

of new management, the airline began to show a profit in the three years to 1993, in preparation for at least a partial privatisation. In 1991 the decision had been made to start retiring the fleet of seven TriStars; they would be replaced by Airbus A340-300s starting in 1994. AirLanka still operates four TriStars in its fleet: two L1011-500s and one each of the L1011-50 and -100, the airline route structure covering Europe as far as London in the West, Tokyo in the East and South Africa.

Cathay was a major operator in the Asian region with a fleet of 14 TriStars but the aircraft was limited to about seven hours flying per day because of the many noise curfews on the routes. Meanwhile, to provide the required regional capacity, three ex-Eastern TriStars were added to the fleet. These required considerable reconfiguration to meet Cathay standards. The maintenance of the 'aging aircraft' did not cause any major problems because of good preventive maintenance. In mid-1989, 10 Airbus A330-300s were ordered to replace the hard working TriStars, and in mid-1990 Cathay

leased a TriStar to Hong Kong-based scheduled and charter operator Dragonair for use on the trunk routes into China; further aircraft was acquired from BA in March 1993. Soon after, the entire fleet of 18 TriStars was sold to Airflee Credit Finance. The withdrawal was to commence from 199 onwards as they were replaced with A330s, with the TriStar being phased out at the rate of five or six per year. Dragonai announced in January 1994 that it would be leasing a pair c Airbus A330s from International Lease Finance Corporatio (ILFC) as replacements for their TriStars leased from

Cathay. Cathay finally retired the last of its 19 TriStars after some 21 years of operation in October 1996. The last commercial service was with TriStar VR-HHY between Nagoya and Taipei on 15 October. On its return to Kai Tak, the aircraft flew a special 45-minute flight around Hong Kong completing 39,754 hours and 20,100 cycles. During its operations with Cathay, the TriStar fleet accumulated just over 487,000 flying hours.

For the busy summer tourist season in 1990 Caledonian Airways, the BA holiday charter subsidiary, increased its TriStar fleet from three aircraft to two L1011-1s, one L1011-50 and two L1011-100s, used mainly on flights to the Mediterranean holiday destinations. At the end of 1994 BA sold its Gatwick-based charter division, Caledonian Airways, to the UK tour-operator group, Inspirations, including five TriStars in the fleet.

In June 1990, Air Canada announced the decision to sell its fleet of 14 TriStars, phasing out eight of the earlier L1011-100s before the end of the year, the last commercial flights of the fleet being at the end of October, following which they were carried to desert storage by the end of November. The remaining long-range L1011-500s used on overseas routes remained in service longer until replaced with Boeing 767-300ERs, deliver-

ies of which were due to start in 1993. However, for the 1994 summer peak season, three TriStars were brought out of storage in the desert and painted in the airline's new livery, to make up a shortage in capacity.

In early 1991, because of the depressed market caused by the Gulf War, British Airways announced that they would be withdrawing their nine L1011-1s from service by May, although the withdrawals started in March, because of the fall in traffic of 20 percent since the start of the war. This would leave eight TriStars in service with BA, with the withdrawn aircraft in desert storage at Mojave, California. By the autumn BA was able to dry-lease two L1011-200s to AirLanka, leaving five aircraft in desert storage at Mojave. The remaining BA TriStars were withdrawn from commercial service by early 1992.

Another casualty of the economic depression caused by the Gulf War was Eastern Airlines, which ceased flying on 18 January 1991, after 22 months of operating under Chapter 11 protection. Its fleet included 16 TriStars at the time, 10 of

BELOW: TotalAir TriStar 1 N702TT, previously served with Delta as N702DA, and was stored in December 1993 as EI-BTN. *Nick Granger*

BOTTOM: Ex-Eastern TriStar 1 N336EA in operation with Worldways of Canada. This aircraft was acquired by Delta in September 1991 as N790DL. *Nick Granger*

TOP: TriStar belonging to Worldways of Canada seen at Newcastle airport in 1989.
Leo Marriott

ABOVE: Rich International TriStar 1 N302MB at London Gatwick on
5 August 1995. This aircraft was retired from ANA as JA8518 in November 1993.
Nick Granger

which were quickly snapped up by Delta in September, along with engines and spares at the auction of bankrupt assets. Delta also acquired some of the ex-Air Canada TriStar 500s in August 1991. Following the start of its services to Gatwick in April 1978, on 18 June 1979 Delta followed up with its eleventh international service from Atlanta to their European hub at Frankfurt. With the demise of PanAm, Delta took over the European routes in November 1991, but it had already been operating TriStar flights to Frankfurt from Atlanta, Cincinnati, Orlando and Dallas. The purchase of the PanAm 'grandfather' rights at Frankfurt allowed Delta to add further transatlantic flights to New York, Miami, Washington DC, Los Angeles and San Francisco, the TriStars sharing the routes with Boeing 767-300ERs. In early 1993, Delta was able to announce its plans to use TriStars to fly daily, non-stop flights from San Francisco to

Frankfurt, starting on 30 June, but in January 1997, the airline reduced drastically its intra-European flights to cut costs; it also planned to develop its profitable transatlantic services. By the end of 1995, Delta was beginning to look at the Airbus A330 and Boeing 777 as replacements for its fleet of 55 TriStars: with aircraft up to 23 years old, Delta were beginning to experience reliability problems. To make use of their combined manufacturing and operating expertise, Delta and Lockheed Martin formed a strategic alliance in early 1996 to offer TriStar maintenance and support to other operators of the aircraft. Delta continued to do its own maintenance at Atlanta and to offer the lighter maintenance to other operators. The Lockheed Martin Aircraft centre at Greenville would perform heavy maintenance, involving structural modifications and repairs. In early 1996 Delta announced its plans to replace the 19 TriStars on the transatlantic services with an additional order for Boeing 767-300ERs, with deliveries in 1997 and 1998. The TriStars made available from these routes were to be reconfigured for replacement of some of the older L1011s in the domestic fleet. Evaluations were continuing into new types for the domestic fleet, but Delta had not announced a timescale.

In 1992, American West, which was also under Chapter 11, leased a TriStar from American Trans Air in late summer to replace its 747s on the non-stop flights to Honolulu from its base at Phoenix. American Trans Air had been formed in August 1973 to operate a Boeing 720, moving from being a travel club to being an airline in 1981. To comply with the new noise regulations being introduced in 1985, ATA purchased an ex-Laker DC-10 in 1983, but the non-availability of further reasonably priced examples resulted in the acquisition of nine ex-Delta TriStars which had been traded into Boeing, deliveries being made during 1985, allowing for the disposal of the DC-10. In 1984 the airline had become a US national carrier, and the substantial increase in fleet size allowed the start of a major charter operation which saw its TriStars operating to Europe, including Gatwick. By 1987 an additional TriStar had been bought, and with further fleet expansion in September 1994, four ex-LTU TriStars were leased from ILFC. The airline has an excellent reputation for a low-cost quality service and keeps two TriStars available on standby, together with two of its Boeing 727s, to maintain its reputation for regularity, particularly with its concentration on future scheduled operations. The aircraft are beginning to appear in a more marketable livery, replacing the previous somewhat conservative design.

Like Eastern, TWA was also operating under the protection of Chapter 11, with plans to recover by mid-1993. In the subsequent reorganisation, the TriStar fleet was expected to reduce to five aircraft, and in fact 12 of the TWA TriStar fleet

BELOW: TAP Air Portugal TriStar 500 CS-TEA leased to Linhas Aereas de Mocambique visiting Gatwick on 10 June 1996. *Nick Granger*

BOTTOM: TriStar 1 EI-TBG with Thorn Browne Group at London Gatwick on 31 July 1996. This early TriStar was originally delivered to TWA as N31010, and later acquired by Air Ops as SE-DPV. Leased from Velvet Aviation in Ireland, it was used frequently as a holiday back-up aircraft during the 1996 season. *Nick Granger*

TOP: Faucett Peru TriStar 50 OB-1545 on approach to Miami on 20 January 1994. This aircraft was originally delivered to TWA as N31021, flying for the final time on 13 September 1992. *Nick Granger*

ABOVE: Worldways Canada TriStar 100 C-GIES was originally built for PSA which accounts for the extra door forward of the wing leading edge in the lower fuselage. This aircraft was seen at London Gatwick on 16 May 1986. *Nick Granger*

RIGHT: TriStar 50 G-CEAP of Atlanta Airways at Gatwick in May 1996 with Air Atlanta TriStar 50 TF-ABM in the background. G-CEAP was originally G-BEAL with BA, British Airtours and Caledonian, before being acquired by AirOps as SE-DPM. *Nick Granger*

were retired to desert storage at the end of October 1992, although a couple were returned to service for the summer peak season the following year. In spring 1994 TWA was restructuring its domestic and international services to improve profitability, which included the replacement of its TriStars with four Boeing 767-300ERs, returning the bulk of the remainder of the fleet to the lessors at the end of October 1994. With its financial recovery, TWA ordered 20 Boeing 757-200s in February 1996 to replace its 14 remaining TriStars, with the first three delivered in 1996 followed by 12 in 1997, the remain-

der of the order following to replace the Boeing 727s. The TriStars had already been withdrawn from the international routes by TWA; and, in fact, it would be replacing a three engine, three-crew aircraft with a twin-engine, two-crew aircraft, saving costs in operation as well as maintenance.

In spring 1993 the TriStar world fleet passed the 10 million flight hour milestone, with some 200 out of the original 250 aircraft still in service. The individual high time was an aircraft delivered to LTU in April 1980, which had logged 61,600 flying hours, and the high-cycle TriStar was delivered to ANA in

TOP: New operator Peach Air with TriStar 1 TF-ABH at Gatwick in May 1997. This aircraft was originally delivered to Eastern as N326EA, later to Cathay Pacific as VR-HHX, who sold it after retirement to Air Atlanta. *Nick Granger*

ABOVE: Air Transat TriStar 100 C-FTNL at London Gatwick on 17 August 1996, having previously seen service with Air Canada until 28 October 1990. *Nick Granger*

BELOW: Many Swedish charter airlines make use of surplus TriStars to carry Scandinavians away from the dark winters to sunnier and warmer climates. This Nordic East TriStar 1 SE-DTC is seen at Rhodes in September 1995 before being sold to Blue Scandinavia at the end of 1996.

July 1975 and had accomplished 31,300 landings on the Japanese busy commuter routes.

Towards the end of 1993 Saudia was considering its future fleet requirements, including a 300-seat replacement for 17 TriStars and 10 Boeing 747-100 aircraft. The replacements were expected to result in an order for up to 23 aircraft, the choice being between the Airbus A330/340, the Boeing 777 and the McDonnell Douglas MD-11, but the decisions were complicated by the urgent need to also acquire aircraft on the 150-seat regional routes, as well as a high-capacity long-range 400-seater, all of which would require a massive investment. Saudia is, therefore, still a major TriStar operator on its regional routes.

BWIA, the Trinidad and Tobago flag carrier, still a TriStar operator today, had a new management team installed in 1993. It managed to bring the airline into profitability, and began looking at the fleet renewal programme in mid-1994. BWIA had four TriStar 500s, of which three would be paid for by June 1995 and would be ready for potential trade-in with replacement aircraft. In November 1995, BWIA selected three Airbus A340s to replace the TriStars from the beginning of 1997.

In the autumn of 1995 Qatar Airways formed a new division to charter and lease aircraft to other carriers in the region, acquiring three TriStars for this purpose in September.

By the middle of 1996 the world TriStar fleet in operation was down to 168 aircraft, but with more in desert storage.

TAP Air Portugal still operate one TriStar 500 CS-TEB mainly on charter flights to Canada, where two of its fleet had been sold to Air Transat, the Canadian charter operator. The remaining two aircraft have been leased, one each to Linhas Aereas de Mocambique (LAM) and TAAG-Angolan Airlines, the TriStars having been replaced by Airbus A340-300s. Air Transat began operating transatlantic TriStars on Canadian to UK charters in the summer season of 1989. The TriStar 500s joined the airline's earlier TriStar 1/150s, both being delivered by mid-January 1997 to provide the necessary non-stop range for the Globespan charter flights from Europe, including Britain to Canada. Also operating TriStars on charter from Canada is an airline called Royal which is committed to providing the ultimate in quality and service. Royal, a Quebec-based airline, was established in January 1992, as an offshoot of Conifair which had been formed in 1979. As well as the Boeing 727-200s used for the shorter range flights out of Montreal and Toronto, Royal operates three TriStars 100s, two ex-Air Canada and one ex-TWA, on the longer range flights to Europe and the Caribbean. An additional ex-TWA TriStar has been acquired for spares' recovery.

With a plentiful supply of surplus high technology TriStars in store after retirement by the major trunk carriers, a number have been put into operation with European charter airlines, which specialise in short term wet-leasing during the busy summer season to the major charter carriers. One of the first companies formed to undertake this work was AirOps of Sweden, which kept some of its fleet of seven TriStars standing

by at Gatwick and Manchester to cover the short-term needs of the established airlines. AirOps started in time for the 199 summer season, but was sold a year later by the ING Bank to become Air Operation International, with one ex-AirOps TriStar and two more leased from the USA. The new AirOps i expected to restart TriStar wet-leases during the 1997 season with SE-DSB, a former TWA aircraft. Also based in Sweden i Blue Scandinavia, formerly Transwede Leisure, which use L1011-1 SE-DTC from Stockholm and Gotenburg to th Greek holiday resorts in the summer, and from Stockholm to the Canary Islands during the winter. The aircraft is also flow on a weekly flight to Stansted. Similar operations to those b AirOps are flown by Iceland-based Air Atlanta, which operate six TriStars for charter to Goldcrest as well as operating scheduled service to Shannon and Dublin, the aircraft some times appearing in the livery of the operator when the lease i over a longer period.

Flying the TriStar

Despite its automatic flight systems, the TriStar aircrews ar enthusiastic about flying the aircraft. In normal passenge operations, the aircraft are flown to a rigid schedule from departure to the destination, although passenger charter and particularly, cargo operations give greater variety. The auto matic systems provide a high level of confidence, and from time to time the autoland can be switched off, to allow the pilots to remain current on how to land the aircraft without the assistance of computers. The TriStar is stable in all fligh regimes, and therefore comfortable for the passengers and crew to travel in.

The pilots who have the real enjoyment of flying the TriStar are the crews of No 216 Squadron based at RAF Brize Norton in Oxfordshire. Although their duties also involve normal international routes, when they operate on air-to-air refuelling sorties, they have to fly the aircraft, much of the time by hand. Once across the airways, the TriStars operate in clea uncontrolled airspace, flying race-track patterns at the various rendezvous points, allowing the thirsty fast jets to top up with fuel. In good weather, the view from the cockpit is excellent and on one particular sortie from Brize Norton, the return flight was made across the Cotswold Hills to overhead the air-field, and then a turn downwind for a visual final approach and landing, much the same as flying a light aircraft. Precise flying of the TriStar makes the task of the refuelled aircraft much easi er in the approach to the hose and drogue, and maintaining contact while sufficient fuel is transferred. See also RAF TriStars.

ABOVE RIGHT: No 216 Squadron TriStar KC Mk 1 ZD953 at around 20,000ft over the North Sea in December 1996, with one of its pair of hose and drogues trailing. *Philip Birtles*

RIGHT: Recent view of a Peach Air TriStar 1 — TF-ABE which was originally delivered to Eastern as N314EA. It is seen loading passengers at Rhodes Airport in August 1997. *Philip Birtles*

6 CUSTOMERS

Air Canada

As part of the Air Holdings commitment to selling the TriStar, Air Canada ordered 10 aircraft in December 1968, with options on nine more, which were eventually confirmed as six of the longer-range L1011-500 in April 1979. The first TriStar was delivered in January 1973 with services commencing the following month on the Toronto–Miami route, later operating on a number of the higher-density long-range domestic services. With their TriStars modified to the -100 standard, Air Canada commenced transatlantic services in April 1977. Air Canada started to phase out eight of the TriStar-100s at the end of 1990, the long range -500s remaining in service until replaced by Boeing 767s in 1993. However, three of the stored TriStars were brought back into service in 1994, to make up a shortage in capacity.

ABOVE LEFT: Air Canada TriStar 100 C-FTNL at Zurich on 26 April 1987. The aircraft flew its last service with Air Canada on 28 October 1990, and is now in service with Air Transat. *Nick Granger*

ABOVE: C-FTNI in desert storage at Marana Arizona in April 1991, following withdrawal from service after its last service on 25 October 1990. This aircraft has now been acquired by Royal of Canada. *Nick Granger*

THIS PICTURE: C-GAGK in March 1991, some 10 years after delivery to the airline. Delta bought the aircraft a year later, reregistering it N769DL. *Leo Marriott*

AirLanka

The final order for new TriStars came from AirLanka in March 1980 for two TriStar 500s, with options on two more. The AirLanka TriStar fleet grew to five aircraft, with two of the -500s still in service, together with one each of the -50 and -100 acquired second-hand.

ABOVE: This TriStar 100 was acquired from All Nippon Airways; registered 4R-ULC it is seen after landing at London Gatwick in December 1987. *Philip Birtles*

BELOW LEFT: Alia TriStar 500 JY-AGH on lease to AirLanka. It has since been sold to Saudi Arabia as HZ-HM6 for use by the Royal Flight. *Nick Granger*

BELOW: L1011-500 4R-ULA seen on final approach to Melbourne. *Bill Lines, via Australian Aviation*

73

TOP: Royal Jordanian TriStar 500 JY-AGH is seen on approach to London Heathrow in October 1988. *Philip Birtles*

ABOVE: Royal Jordanian TriStar 500 JY-AGD at London Gatwick on 1 February 1987 in the airline's new livery. *Nick Granger*

RIGHT: Alia Royal Jordanian TriStar 500 JY-AGD in the original livery at London Heathrow on 10 November 1985. The aircraft is still with the airline. *Nick Granger*

TOP RIGHT: ANA TriStar 1s JA8521 and JA8522 are seen ready for departure. Since being withdrawn from service, both aircraft are with Rich International. *ANA*

FAR RIGHT: TriStar 1 JA8521 is an example of the ANA use of the aircraft on international routes, on this occasion Hong Kong. All the TriStars have now been withdrawn from the airline and this particular aircraft was acquired by Rich International and is currently stored. *Rob Finlayson via Australian Aviation*

Alia Royal Jordanian Airlines

Ordered five TriStars at the end of 1979, with four more added later, including one for the Jordanian Royal Flight. These TriStars were required for the European and transatlantic routes, and five continue in operation today, in addition to the one with the Royal Flight.

All Nippon Airways

Options placed for six TriStars in March 1971, the aircraft to be used on the high density domestic routes, particularly between Osaka and Tokyo. The ANA order for six TriStars was confirmed in October 1972, with options on a further 15 aircraft, with 10 being confirmed by the end of 1973. ANA increased its commitment for TriStars in September 1974 by a further seven aircraft, and in April 1977 made its fleet up to 20 TriStars. All have now been withdrawn from service.

British Airways

The British Government announced its approval for BEA, later to become part of BA, to buy TriStars in August 1972, the initial order being for six standard-range TriStars for the European routes, and to be followed by six extended-range aircraft for Middle Eastern destinations. When BEA signed the contract on 26 September the options had been increased to 12 aircraft, and in October 1973 the firm orders were increased to nine TriStars, with a further nine still on option. The first TriStar was delivered to BA on 21 October 1974 with the first commercial service on 12 January 1975, by which time firm TriStar orders for BA were 15 aircraft. In January 1979 BA ordered their first two TriStar 200s, adding six more in September 1979, bringing its total to 23 aircraft.

BA placed the launch order for the long-range TriStar 500 in August 1976, by converting six of its earlier options, and adding a further six options. These aircraft were ideal for the long-range, thin routes, as far as the US West Coast from London, and the first one entered service in May 1979.

BA began the withdrawal of its TriStar fleet in spring 1991, because of the loss of passengers caused by the Gulf War, and by early 1992 all were out of service, either in desert storage, or being converted to freighters for civil operation in the case of the L1011-200s, and tanker/transports for the RAF, in the case of the -500s.

BELOW: L1011-500 G-BLUS was originally AirLanka's *City of Colombo*. BA leased the aircraft 1985-88. *British Airways*

BOTTOM: BA TriStar 500 G-BLUT, which was on lease from AirLanka, seen at Heathrow on 10 November 1985. It has since returned to AirLanka as 4R-ULB. *Nick Granger*

RIGHT: BEA, later to become part of British Airways, placed its first order for TriStars in August 1972. The initial order, worth £20 million, was for six TriStar 1s, with options on six more aircraft. These early TriStars were intended for the high density European routes. Here is L1011-1 G-BBAH on approach to Heathrow in February 1988, by then in the colours of BA; later it would become part of the Caledonian fleet. *Philip Birtles*

BELOW RIGHT: G-BHBM taking-off. Note undercarriage retraction. *Leo Marriott*

British West Indian Airways

In September 1978 BWIA ordered two TriStar 500s, with two options, for Caribbean–London services, the first being delivered in January 1980. The two options were converted into orders in September 1980, and the aircraft are still used on the European routes, although they are due to be phased out in 1997, as they are replaced by Airbus A340s.

LEFT: TriStar 500 9Y-THA was delivered in November 1981. *Rolls-Royce*

BELOW LEFT: N3140D seen in 1990. *Leo Marriott*

BELOW: BWIA ordered three Airbus A340s in November 1995 to replace its TriStars from early 1997. Towards the end of its career with the airline, L1011-500 9Y-TGN is seen about to depart from London Heathrow in November 1996. *Philip Birtles*

Cathay Pacific

In March 1974 Cathay signed a letter of intent for two extended-range TriStars, with options on two more, the aircraft to be used on the Asian routes from its base at Hong Kong. The Cathay Pacific fleet of TriStars eventually grew to 14 new aircraft, being operated on a very high utilisation, and later having three ex-Eastern TriStars join the airline. The withdrawal of the TriStars commenced in 1995, with the gradual replacement by Airbus A330s, until the last TriStar service was flown on 15 October 1996.

TOP: Cathay TriStar 100 VR-HHK is seen touching down on the runway at Hong Kong. Following its retirement it has been registered N155MC. *Scott Allen, via Australian Aviation*

ABOVE: L-1011-1 N316EA was initially leased and then bought by Cathay from Eastern. It flew as VR-HOB until 11 May 1996 when it was bought by Transat. *Cathay Pacific*

ABOVE RIGHT: Court Line's second TriStar 1, G-BAAB, was named *Halcyon Breeze* and delivered to Luton in April 1973, but was grounded in August 1974. It was acquired by Cathay Pacific in October 1977 and is currently operated by Air Atlanta of Iceland. *Philip Birtles*

Court Line

In November 1971, the first British order for TriStars came from this Luton-based company: it was for two aircraft for the 1973 tourist summer season, followed by three options to be delivered one per year from 1974 onwards. The aircraft were to be used entirely for holiday charter flights to the Mediterranean resorts. The contract was finally signed on 12 August 1972, and the first aircraft was delivered to Luton on 5 March 1973 with the first service to Palma on 2 April. Because of difficulties caused by the fuel crisis, Court Line ceased operations on 15 August 1974, its two TriStars later being acquired by Cathay.

Delta

An early customer for the TriStar, it placed an order for 24 aircraft with deliveries planned to commence in 1972. The first TriStar was in fact delivered to Delta on 3 October 1973.

BELOW: By the end of 1995 Delta was experiencing increased maintenance costs with its ageing TriStar fleet of 56 aircraft, and had to consider replacement. Older aircraft were replaced by the younger TriStar 500s, themselves replaced on transatlantic services by Boeing 767-300ERs. L1011-250 N740DA is seen about to depart from London Gatwick in August 1995. *Philip Birtles*

Initially using the aircraft on domestic routes from its hub at Atlanta, Delta later acquired longer-range Series 200s to allow the start of transatlantic operations, which were subsequently operated by the long-range Series 500, when it became available. Delta continued to top up its TriStar fleet until production ceased and acquired additional aircraft from the bankrupt Eastern and retired aircraft from Air Canada. Delta ordered its first long-range TriStar 500s in January 1978, for its transatlantic routes. With a current fleet of around 56 TriStars, amongst its other aircraft, Delta has recently decided on replacements in the form of the new stretched Boeing 767-400, together with some Boeing 777s. As well as operating on US domestic routes, and transatlantic, Delta also took over many of the Frankfurt-centred European services previously operated by PanAm, but these have now been withdrawn.

RIGHT: Eastern TriStar 1 N332EA just after take-off with the undercarriage beginning to retract. This aircraft is now operated by Delta as N786DL. *Nick Granger*

BELOW RIGHT: On 17 May 1971 the third TriStar, N301EA, joined the flight test fleet, and was eventually delivered to Eastern on 22 May 1973 as N302EA. It was bought by Delta in June 1991, and ended up as a Lockheed ground test specimen in October 1995. *Lockheed*

BELOW: N1739D was delivered to Delta in December 1982 and converted from -1 to -250 status in December 1986. *Leo Marriott*

BOTTOM: Delta continued to increase its fleet of TriStars bringing its total to 25 aircraft by the end of 1978. Delta TriStar 1 N788DL, operating from Atlanta in December 1992 was acquired from Eastern in September 1991. *Philip Birtles*

Eastern Airlines

One of the launch customers for the TriStar, it placed its initial order and options for 50 TriStars on 29 March 1968. The first TriStar was handed over to Eastern at the beginning of April 1972 for crew training, allowing commercial services to commence on 26 April from Miami to New York. The TriStars were used by Eastern on its domestic high density routes, the three engines giving a greater safety level on some of the over-sea flights down the east coast of the US. Because the economic depression caused a drop in traffic figures, Eastern eventually only took delivery of 30 TriStars, some of which were disposed to other airlines soon after. Eastern finally went into liquidation on 18 January 1991, after 22 months of operating under the protection of Chapter 11. All its aircraft were grounded, a number being acquired by Delta.

Gulf Air

Ordered four extended-range L1011-100s with options on a further four in December 1974, for operations across Europe. Gulf Air added two L1011-200s in August 1979, with a seventh aircraft added the following spring. Gulf Air eventually operated a total of 11 TriStars, of various types, but in mid-1992 announced plans to sell up to eight TriStars, to help raise the finance for newly ordered Boeing 767s. Five TriStar 200s remained in storage, and with the sale of five of the new Boeing 767s to Delta, Gulf Air brought three of the TriStars back into service in the 1997 season.

RIGHT AND BELOW: Two views of A40-TT, a -200 delivered in December 1981. *Leo Marriott*

BELOW RIGHT: In spring 1989 Gulf Air ordered six extended-range Boeing 767-300ERs as the start of the process of replacing its TriStars. Although they were all withdrawn by 1996, three stored aircraft were returned to service for the 1997 season, one of them being A40-TB seen on approach to London Heathrow in June 1991. *Philip Birtles*

ABOVE: LTU TriStar over Gatwick in March 1985. Note undercarriage doors retracting. *Leo Marriott*

ABOVE LEFT: LTU TriStar 1 D-AERY at Majorca on 26 January 1987. It was acquired by American Transair as N178AT, and withdrawn from use in January 1995 for spares' recovery. *Nick Granger*

LEFT: In October 1972 the Dusseldorf-based airline placed its initial order for two TriStars with all-economy layouts for 330 passengers. This TriStar 1, D-AERA, later went to Eastern as N372EA, then Cathay; it is now with Transwede as SE-DTD. *Lockheed*

LTU

In October 1972, this German holiday charter airline signed a letter of intent for two TriStars to be used on holiday flights to the Mediterranean resorts, the first aircraft being delivered to the airline on 29 May 1973, later exchanging these aircraft for three ex PSA aircraft. LTU also ordered two TriStar 500s in May 1979 for the longer range charter flights.

Northeast

Placed orders for a total of six TriStars, plus four options, but before they could be delivered, the airline was taken over by Delta.

TOP: Another view of N10114 at Farnborough in 1974. *Philip Birtles*

ABOVE: Pacific Southwest Airlines' aircraft were configured with a lower-deck lounge, and therefore a prominent protective skid was fitted under the fuselage in the event of a wheels up landing. The first PSA TriStar, N10112, passed to the Canadian operator Worldways, and has now been modified into a flying hospital for Operation 'Blessing'. *Lockheed*

Pacific Southwest Airlines

PSA issued a letter of intent for two TriStars, and reservation on a further three aircraft, on the day of the roll-out of the firs TriStar on 1 September 1970. PSA needed the TriStars for it high density California routes, particularly between Lo Angeles and San Francisco. After some delays because of eco nomic difficulties with the airline, PSA was able to confirm i order for five TriStars in September 1972, and the first one wa delivered to the airline in July 1974. With the fuel crisis devel oping in 1976, PSA had to ground its two TriStars in servic while the next batch of three remained undelivered at Palmdal they were later acquired by LTU.

PanAm

Became a new TriStar customer in April 1978 with an order for 12 TriStar 500s, plus options on a further 14 aircraft. The airline commenced services with the TriStars in July 1980. PanAm ceased operations in November 1991, and three of its TriStar 500s were ferried to Marshall Aerospace at Cambridge for conversion to military transports for the RAF.

ABOVE: PanAm TriStar 500 N509PA which is now in service with No 216 Squadron, RAF at Lyneham, having been converted to C2A ZE705. *Nick Granger*

BELOW: PanAm's TriStars were fitted with extended wingtips and active ailerons. PanAm TriStar 500 N514PA was delivered in December 1981, and is seen at Zurich in March 1983. When United took over some of the PanAm routes in February 1986, this aircraft joined United, and has now joined the Delta fleet as N762DA. *Philip Birtles*

Saudia

Initial order placed for two extended-range TriStars, with three options in March 1974, adding two of the longer range L1011-200s for its European routes in September 1974. The first Saudia TriStar was delivered in July 1975 with services commencing on 15 August, and three more TriStar 200s were ordered in September 1977, with the fleet increasing to 13 TriStars by May 1978. Saudia remains a major TriStar operator, although plans are in hand to replace the fleet with more modern types.

TOP LEFT: Saudia TriStar 200 HZ-AHG at London Heathrow on 6 March 1983. *Nick Granger*

LEFT: Saudia TriStar 200 HZ-AHM which was delivered to the airline in October 1979 seen on push-back at Zurich around 1986. *Philip Birtles*

TOP: The Saudia order in September 1974 launched the extended higher performance TriStar into service, powered by RB211-524 engines. L1011-200 HZ-AHG is seen operating from London Heathrow and is still in service with the airline. *Philip Birtles*

ABOVE: Saudia TriStar 200 HZ-AHB first flew on 28 June 1975, was delivered on 12 July and is still in operation with the airline. *Saudia*

TAP Air Portugal

Became a new TriStar customer in September 1979, when it ordered three TriStar 500s, with options on two more, which were later converted to firm orders. TAP used the aircraft on its longer-range routes, but by early 1997 it only maintained one in operation, for long-range charters to north America, two having been sold to Air Transat in Canada, and the other two leased out to other operators.

TOP: L1011-500 CS-TEF at Zurich on 19 March 1992. Previously with Alia as JY-AGJ, it is currently leased to Air India as V2-LEJ. *Nick Granger*

ABOVE: By 1997 TAP was only operating one of its original five -500s, two having been sold to Air Transat and the other two leased out. TriStar 500 CS-TEC was delivered to TAP in March 1983 and is currently leased to TAAG. *TAP*

BELOW: TAP Air Portugal TriStar 500 CS-TEE is seen on approach to London Heathrow in May 1992 and was sold to Air Transat in January 1997. *Philip Birtles*

TWA

The joint launch airline with Eastern for the TriStar, TWA announced a commitment for 44 aircraft on 29 March 1968. These aircraft were mainly required for the US transcontinental routes, the three engines giving a safety margin over the Rockies. TWA took delivery of the first TriStar in early May 1972, and flew the inaugural service on 25 June. TWA later put some of its TriStars in transatlantic operations, starting in spring 1978. Out of the total of eventually 37 TriStars, a small number remain in operation on domestic routes in the USA. TWA plans to replace its TriStars with Boeing 757s when finances allow.

ABOVE RIGHT: L1011-200 N31033 at London Gatwick on 14 June 1988. It was returned the following year to Saudia as HZ-AHF, where it is still in operation. *Nick Granger*

RIGHT: During 1997 TWA finally retired its TriStars from US domestic services, replacing the last 14 aircraft with 20 Boeing 757-200s. Here, L1011-50 N31018 is seen on approach to London Heathrow in June 1989. It was sold to AirOps as SE-DSC and used for spares before scrapping at Hurn in September 1990. *Philip Birtles*

BELOW: The second TriStar, N31001, although destined for Eastern, made its maiden flight on 15 February 1971 in the markings of TWA. Later used by Faucett, it was dismantled for spares' recovery at Miami in May 1994. *Lockheed*

SECOND OWNER AIRLINES

BELOW: Air Atlanta Icelandic TriStar 1 TF-ABH at London Gatwick on 31 May 1996. *Nick Granger*

BOTTOM: AirOps TriStar 50 SE-DPP at London Gatwick on 11 March 1995 still in the basic Hawaiian colours. It is now with Air Atlanta as TF-ABM. *Nick Granger*

Air Atlanta of Iceland has a fleet of six TriStars used for charter and wet-lease to fill capacity gaps with the established operators.

AirOps of Sweden operated a fleet of seven TriStars, mainly on wet-lease to the established operators, when there was a capacity shortfall during the busy summer season. A number of its fleet were kept on standby at Manchester and Gatwick, but the airline ceased operations in 1996, when it was sold by the bank providing the finance.

TOP: This TriStar 50 was originally delivered to TWA as N31024, before it was acquired by Hawaiian, whose basic livery it still carries. The aircraft was stored before a repaint in Air Atlanta colours for the start of the 1997 season. *Philip Birtles*

ABOVE: AirOps TriStar 100 SE-DSD was originally N31032 with TWA which retired it after its last service on 25 October 1992, and is seen here ready for departure at Gatwick in July 1995. It was put into storage in 1996. *Philip Birtles*

TOP: TriStar 500 C-GTSQ, seen at Gatwick in March 1997. *Nick Granger*

ABOVE: C-FTNA was originally the first TriStar 1 delivered to Air Canada, and is seen at the London Gatwick holding point in August 1995. *Philip Birtles*

Air Transat began operating TriStars on transatlantic charter from Canada to Europe in 1989, adding a pair of ex-TAl TriStar 500s in early 1997.

American Trans Air acquired nine ex-Delta TriStars in 1985 for long-range international charter operations, mainly to European destinations, as well as domestic US routes. By 1994 the TriStar fleet had grown to 14 aircraft, which continue in operation.

ABOVE: American Trans Air was formed as a holiday club in August 1973 and became a US national carrier in 1984. TriStar 50 N187AT was delivered to the airline in April 1985, having previously been N707DA with Delta. *Marshall Aerospace*

BELOW: Another view of N186AT, this time at London Gatwick on 17 September 1996 in the new livery. This aircraft had previously operated with Delta as N706DA. *Nick Granger*

ABOVE: The only TriStar operated by Blue Scandinavia is registered SE-DTC.

Blue Scandinavia operates one TriStar 1 from Sweden to the Greek holiday resorts, starting in 1997.

BELOW: Caledonian G-BEAL, originally delivered to BA in 1976. *Leo Marriott*

BOTTOM: G-BBAF made its last revenue flight with BA on 5 November 1990. It is seen here on finals to Rhodes in 1995. *Philip Birtles*

Caledonian Airways, originally the holiday charter subsidiary of BA, operates five TriStars, and was sold to Inspirations at the end of 1994. It continues to operate the TriStars on the Mediterranean holiday destination routes from its main base at Gatwick and other regional airports.

RAF The first of five ex-BA TriStar 500s was delivered to the RAF as a tanker/transport aircraft in March 1986 for service with No 216 Squadron, followed by three of the passenger-configured ex-PanAm TriStar 500s. All remain in service.

TOP: KC1 ZD950 works as a tanker/transporter for the RAF. *Philip Birtles*

ABOVE: Canadian-based Royal C-FTNI is one of three TriStars in the company. *Philip Birtles*

Royal This Canadian-based company was started in January 1992, and operates three TriStars on transatlantic charter operations.

United After the demise of PanAm in November 1991, United got six TriStar 500s for short-term operation.

Below: N514PA was bought from PanAm by United. *United*

CARGO CONVERSIONS

BELOW: TriStar 200F N102CK at Cambridge after conversion with the cargo door in the full vertical position. *Marshall Aerospace*

BOTTOM: American International Airways TriStar 200 N108CK at Gatwick on 17 May 1997. This TriStar had not been converted to a cargo configuration, and was being used for passenger charter flights. *Nick Granger*

American International Airways placed the launch order for the TriStar 200 cargo conversion in July 1994, for three firm aircraft, and options on a further five.

LEFT: The C4A cargo door fitted to the civil conversions of the TriStar 200 is shown on the Arrow conversion of N306GB. *Marshall Aerospace*

BELOW: In early 1995 International Air Leases placed an order for three TriStar 200Fs to be operated by Miami-based Arrow Air. TriStar 200F N306GB is seen at Cambridge before delivery. *Marshall Aerospace*

BOTTOM: International Lease Finance ordered one TriStar 200F N851MA for Millon Air of Miami. *Marshall Aerospace*

International Air Leases (IAL) ordered three TriStar 200 freighters for Miami-based **Arrow Air** in early 1995, adding a further aircraft for **Millon Air** in 1996.

ODDBALLS AND ODDITIES

Flying Hospital

Lockheed Martin Aircraft Services announced in mid-1995 the plans to convert a TriStar into a flying hospital for Operation 'Blessing', International Relief and Development. The converted aircraft was the largest self-contained flying hospital ever built. The main deck was fitted out with an operating theatre, a pre/post operating section, surgical preparation area and a patient examination room. The main deck also houses two dental and ear-nose-and-throat treatment rooms. The lower deck was fitted with a pharmacy, check in/check out reception, galley, and the crew rest area which doubled as a medical consultancy room. The new interior and equipment was installed over a period of 10 months at the Lockheed Aeromod Centre in Tucson, Arizona. With the aircraft to operate on station for at least a week at a time, it was fitted with its own auxiliary ground power units and a water purification system. Conversion was completed by mid-1996 of the L1011-50 ready for its duties of providing medical relief in Latin America, Eastern Europe and Asia.

MARSHALL AEROSPACE

TriStar tanker conversions

Marshall Aerospace is a long-established family-run high quality engineering organisation based at Cambridge in England. It has for many years been the design authority for the Lockheed C-130 Hercules, providing complete support for the fleet in service with the RAF and undertaking major work for many military and other operators of these aircraft. The company, therefore, had good working relationships with the Lockheed Martin Corporation, which continues through the support of the TriStar both in conversions for military use, commercial freighters and major maintenance for the current airline operators.

Marshall Aerospace first became involved with the TriStar, when, after the Falklands Campaign, the British Government was looking for a long-range high-capacity transport and flight-refuelling tanker aircraft, to be able to resupply rapidly some of the more remote parts of the world under British protection. Discussions commenced in September 1982, when the options were between modifying surplus British Caledonian DC-10s or the British Airways TriStars. The requirement was for the

LEFT: Following experience with the TriStar conversions for the RAF, where the cargo doors and surrounds were jig-built separately, Marshall adapted the civil cargo conversions where the airframe was fully supported and the cargo door surround structure built into the airframe directly. *Marshall Aerospace*

ABOVE: Following completion of the cargo door surround structure, the cargo door s lifted into place. This unit is produced under sub-contract by British Aerospace Aerostructures at Manchester. *Marshall Aerospace*

tanker aircraft to be able to carry an additional 45 tons of fuel in special tanks in the underfloor cargo bay, with a pair of hose drum units (HDU) at the rear, to provide for 'fail-safe' when operating away on a deployment. The tanker was also to be capable of carrying up to 44 tons of cargo or up to 204 seats, or a combination of both, on the main deck.

With its associations with Lockheed, it was logical for Marshall to tender for the conversion of the six surplus British Airways TriStar 500s, while British Aerospace and British Caledonian tendered for the DC-10 conversion with the backing of McDonnell Douglas. The British Government insisted on a fixed price incentive contract, leaving the winning contractor with a high level of risk. It was the biggest retrofit programme to be undertaken on any aircraft, with the new problems of housing the 45 tons of fuel not only in the cargo bay of the aircraft, but also within the pressure shell. Because the conversion started with the first four aircraft almost simultaneously, with no prototype, any rework required as experience was gained on the first aircraft would have to be repeated in the same areas on the follow-on aircraft. Modifications would also be required of the new equipment and systems as the ground testing progressed, including the complete new fuel system. This was all in addition to the structural challenges of cutting a large cargo door for the first time in the second-hand TriStars.

On 2 February the contract was placed with Marshall. The conversion was handled in three phases, with the first four being completed as K Mk 1 tanker/passenger aircraft, but without a cargo door. The first made its maiden flight from Cambridge on 9 July 1985. The first two were delivered to an interim standard, while the next two were to the full K Mk 1 standard. The fifth and sixth aircraft were to the complete KC Mk 1 standard with an upper-deck cargo door, with the first two interim aircraft returning later for conversion to the full KC Mk 1 standard.

The purchase in 1984 of the three TriStar 500 aircraft from PanAm brought a further complication because, although they were generally similar, detail differences meant that they could not be converted to the same tanker standard, and in the end they were allocated as purely passenger carrying aircraft, giving No 216 Squadron three standards of aircraft in its fleet consisting of two tanker/passenger-carrying K Mk 1s, four tanker/cargo/passenger-carrying KC Mk 1s and three purely passenger-carrying C Mk 2s. Plans were made to convert the ex-PanAm aircraft to the first three-point tankers with hose drums under the outer wings, followed later by the ex-British Airways aircraft, but although the option still exists, it is not in any current programme.

TriStar ZD950 was used by Marshall for flight development to clear hose drum modifications and the new avionics equipment before going to Boscombe Down for the first half of 1988 to clear the air-to-air flight refuelling capability with all

RIGHT: Marshall Aerospace at Cambridge has built an excellent reputation for support of the TriStar, as well as for a number of other aircraft types. A Caledonian TriStar is seen on a maintenance programme, with an RAF TriStar in the background. Marshall currently has a contract to provide all the heavy maintenance for the RAF TriStar fleet. *Marshall Aerospace*

BELOW: The civil cargo TriStars are fitted with a 9g cargo restraint bulkhead at the forward end of the cabin, and between it and the flightdeck bulkhead are two rows of triple seats on the starboard side for the use of couriers. *Marshall Aerospace*

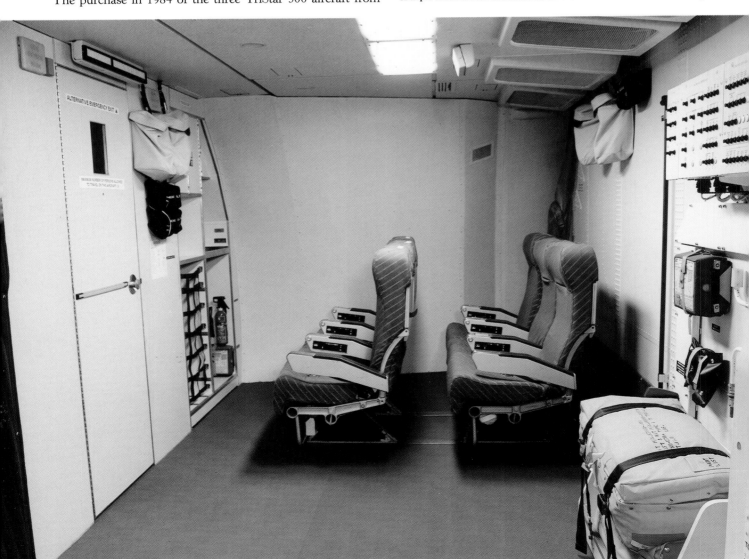

the anticipated receiver aircraft. Meanwhile the first TriStar configured as a tanker, ZD953, was handed over by Marshall to the RAF on 24 March 1986, thus becoming the RAF's first multi-role air-to-air refuelling tanker/transport, and the first wide-bodied aircraft to be operated by any air force outside the USA. By the end of the year three K Mk 1 TriStars were in service with the RAF, and the first two conversions were being made to ZD948 and ZD952 to the full cargo configuration.

The C.4 cargo installation consisted of an upper deck upward opening door measuring 11ft 8in (3.6m) by 8ft 6in (2.6m) and installed on the port side of the cabin. The first conversion was to ZD948.

BA Sunset III conversions

Having gained experience with the TriStar, Marshall was able successfully to tender for the contract with British Airways to complete what was known as the Sunset III conversion. Starting with G-BHBR, the work was on 10 of the longer range L.1011-50s and L.1011-200s and consisted mainly of moving the lower-deck galleys to the passenger deck to make more space for freight and baggage in the hold, and to reconfigure and refurbish the passenger cabins.

Cargo conversions

Marshall realised that, with the entry into service of the new generation of airliners, many of the TriStars, still with a useful economic life in them, could be converted to dedicated cargo aircraft for much less than it would cost to buy a new aircraft. It could use not only its knowledge of the TriStar, but also the expertise gained in installing the cargo doors on the RAF aircraft. This commercial freighter programme is fully supported by the Lockheed Martin Aeronautical Systems and, depending upon the operators' requirements, a total of up to 23 7ft 4in (2.25m) by 10ft 5in (3.2m) pallets can be carried in the main cabin with 16 LD-3 containers up to a weight of 36,000lb (16,400kg) in the forward hold, and a further eight containers, weighing up to 18,000lb (8,200) in the rear hold.

The TriStar version chosen for this programme was the Series 200 increasing the maximum gross take-off weight from 466,000lb (212,000kg) to 474,000lb (215,000kg).

Marshall has the capacity to complete up to three freighter conversions at any one time and should additional business be achieved, Lockheed Martin in Greenville North Carolina has the capacity to complete two further conversions. Lockheed Air Services has completed one cargo conversion for Tradewinds in

the US. The major challenge at the moment for Marshall is to reduce the down time of the aircraft, the target being 18 to 22 weeks depending on the customer specification, including any additional work required in terms of mandatory modifications, service bulletins and structural repairs.

The civil cargo versions were launched when American International Airways placed an order for three conversions of -200 TriStars in July 1994, with options for a further five aircraft. A batch of ex-British Airways aircraft were allocated to this programme, and by the end of 1996 10 aircraft had either been converted and entered into service, or were in the conversion programme. In early 1995 an order was placed by International Air Leases (IAL) for three conversions of ex-Gulf Air TriStar 200s, with further options. The three firm orders for these aircraft are in operation with Arrow Air based at Miami. In addition the ILFC have ordered one -200 freighter conversion for Millon Air, also of Miami, with an ex-LTU aircraft being used on this occasion.

Satellite launcher

The other major TriStar modification undertaken by Marshall was for the Orbital Sciences Pegasus rocket-powered satellite launcher. The main object was to find a launch platform for satellites that was practical and more affordable. The TriStar has been adapted to carry the Pegasus vehicle for an in flight launch at 38,000ft (11,600m), the largest free-fall unmanned object ever dropped from an aircraft. An ex-Air Canada L1011-1-15 had the lower deck galley removed and most of the passenger cabin stripped out, permanently sealing the doors that would not be required. A support and release system was built in the wing box centre-section between the first and third spars, which did not accommodate fuel on this version.

The Pegasus airframe has a high stub wing which fits under the aircraft fuselage, with an anhedral tailplane and the fin recessed into the underside of the TriStar. Launch of the vehicle is slightly nose-up to give clearance of the fin when it is released. The TriStar selected for this programme was fairly young in terms of operation with 45,000hr/15,000 landings in commercial operation, and therefore the only part of the ageing aircraft programme required was to replace the belly skins fore and aft of the wing.

The modified aircraft made its maiden flight from Cambridge on 12 July 1993 and on its sixth flight just under a month later it carried a dummy Pegasus for the first time. Apart from the obvious increase in drag, the general handling qualities of the TriStar were unaffected. However, when the Pegasus is released, there is a substantial rearward movement of the centre of gravity, close to the rear of its acceptable range. To counter the additional drag, the RB211 engines were tuned to give a 10 percent increase in power. Following completion of the flight trials and delivery of the TriStar to Orbital Sciences the Pegasus made its first successful powered launch on 3 April 1995.

Overhauls

As well as these TriStar conversions, and its other aerospace work Marshall has also done a number of major overhauls and modifications to the normal in-service aircraft with the airlines. Although there are no long term formal contracts, the TriStar expertise built up over the years is recognised and aircraft from the fleets of LTU, Caledonian, Royal Jordanian, BWIA, American Trans Air, Saudia, Gulf Air and others have been regular visitors to Hangar 17 at Cambridge.

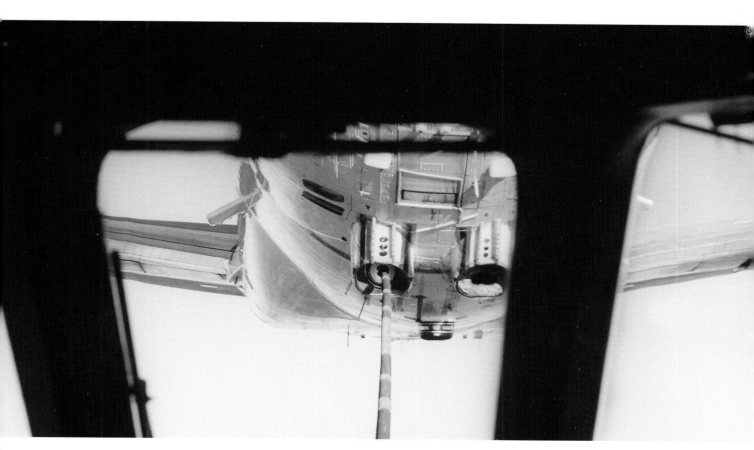

ABOVE LEFT: The flightdeck of No 216 Squadron TriStar ZD953 with the captain on the left and the co-pilot on the right. The controls and instrumentation for the three Rolls-Royce RB211 engines are on the centre console. *Philip Birtles*

LEFT: The flight engineer's panel on ZD953 on the starboard side of the cockpit behind the co-pilot. This is where the aircraft systems are controlled, including the monitoring of the fuel being supplied to the receiver aircraft, the major instrumentation change for No 216 Squadron being the TV screen at the bottom right for viewing the actual contact. It's interesting to compare this picture to the civil flight engineer's station on page 37. *Philip Birtles*

ABOVE: The No 10 Squadron VC-10 plugs into the port hose and drogue of ZD953 in December 1996 in a training exercise over the North Sea. Just behind the hose units, it is said, is the slot where the Tornado pilots reach up to wipe through their credit card when paying for the fuel. *Philip Birtles*

RIGHT: The flight engineer's TV screen gives a view through 180 degrees from each wing trailing edge, monitoring the approach, refuelling and departure of the receiving aircraft. On the screen in this view is a Tornado F3 taking on fuel from the port hose and drogue. *Philip Birtles*

ABOVE: The stark interior of the TriStar KC1 with the overhead bins removed to give the maximum clearance for cargo. The forward-facing seats, galley units and cargo area are all mounted on pallets to allow the full flexibility of loading for all passenger to all cargo configuration, or any combination in between. When cargo is carried the restraining net is lowered. This is the interior of ZD953 in December 1996 after fitting the upper-deck cargo door. *Philip Birtles*

RIGHT: KC ZD953 of No 216 Squadron supplying fuel to a No 29 Squadron Tornado F3 while Tornados from Nos 25 and 43 Squadrons wait their turn. *RAF Brize Norton*

door. As with many other units in the RAF, No 216 Squadron was busy on Operation 'Granby' to combat the occupation of Kuwait by Iraq. Two of the aircraft were deployed to Riyadh in Saudi Arabia, painted an overall pink as a desert camouflage. The K1s flew over 90 air-to-air refuelling missions totalling over 430 hours during the Gulf War. The other TriStars with No 216 were used to provide transport and support for the troops and aircraft deployed to the Gulf, operating from Britain, Cyprus and Germany. From June 1993 to July 1994 the two K1s were based at Milan Airport in support of the UN aircraft operating over the former Yugoslavia, and have now moved to Palermo in support of the NATO Peace Keeping Force in the region.

The next four ex-British Airways TriStar 500s were modified by Marshall to the full tanker/transport standard as KC1s with the large main deck cargo door — ZD948, ZD950, ZD952 and ZD953. These four aircraft are used regularly on flight refuelling sorties from Brize Norton, mainly out over the North Sea from Scotland to The Wash, as well as the trooping runs twice a week to the Falklands, once or twice a week to Cyprus, which is accomplished in one long day, as well as supporting the competing RAF aircraft and crews for the annual Red Flag exercise in California. There is also a weekly flight to Split in support of IFOR in the Balkans, and regular support to annual exercises, 'Pond Jump West' being held in the summer in Edmonton, Canada. There is also support provided for the army exercises, in the summer to Calgary in Canada for 'Medicine Man' and the winter to Nairobi for 'Grand Prix'.

The remaining three ex-PanAm TriStar 500s, ZE704, ZE705 and ZE706, are C Mk 2s which can carry up to 250 passengers.

7 ATTRITION

LEFT: The wreckage of N310EA lies shattered and scattered over the Florida Everglades. *Associated Press*

'whatever happens keep flying the aircraft', and the undercarriage problem took the crew's attention away from monitoring the performance of the TriStar. While the captain was trying to change the bulb, the first officer was monitoring the operation of the autopilot, which as far as he could tell was still switched on. The TriStar has a trap door in the cockpit floor which allows inspection in the 'hell hole' of the avionics bay, and also has a periscope which allows the visual check of the nosewheel undercarriage. Don Repo, assisted by Angelo Donadeo, went down through this hatch to try and check the nosewheel position, and by leaving the engineer's station failed to hear the quiet warning chime signi-

Eastern Airlines' N310EA

The TriStar gained a good reputation for safety during its operational life, but like all aircraft has suffered some regrettable accidents. It also had the dubious honour of being the first of the wide-bodied jet airliners to crash. TriStar N310EA was delivered to Eastern Airlines on 18 August 1972 and was allocated to Flight 401 on 29 December 1972 from New York to Miami with a load of 163 passengers and 13 crew members. On the flightdeck was Captain Bob Loft, First Officer Bert Stockstill, Flight Engineer Don Repo and an Eastern Airlines engineer, Angelo Donadeo, riding in the jump seat.

The flight was routine until the approach to Miami, when the undercarriage was selected down for the landing, and the nosewheel locked-down indicator light failed to illuminate. In a precautionary move, the crew overshot the airport, climbing to 2,000ft (600m) while the problem was investigated. One of the first and simplest things they tried was to change the bulb to determine if it was just an indicator error, and when leaning forward one of the pilots inadvertently knocked the control column, which — unknown to them — disengaged the autopilot and put the aircraft in a gradual descent. There is a well known pilots' saying —

fying the start of the descent. The captain and first officer had their attention diverted by a $10 light bulb.

Because of the darkness outside over the Everglades swamps, the crew had no visual reference and neither pilot could see the other's instrument panel. Just as Don Repo was able to look down the optics for the nose-leg, he saw a reflection of the nosewheel light in the waters of the swamp, and before he could shout a warning, the aircraft hit the ground in a level attitude 17 miles (27km) west of Miami International Airport, breaking up on impact. Although the crash was considered unsurvivable, the strong structure of the wide-bodied jet airliner absorbed some of the shock of impact resulting in the survival of 76 of the 176 people on board. Bob Loft was still alive in the wreckage of the flight deck, but died before the rescue services could get him out. The first officer, Bert Stockstill was killed in the impact. However in the 'hell hole' under the remains of the cockpit floor, both Don Repo and Angelo Donadeo were alive, but injured, Don Repo dying a few days later in hospital. Angelo Donadeo survived and was able to assist significantly in the subsequent accident investigation.

The black boxes were recovered, the flight data recorder indicating the gradual rate of descent just before impact and mongst the conversations on the flightdeck the cockpit voice recorder also picked up the chime of the descent warning. The accident report issued by the US National Transport Safety Board (NTSB) attributed the prime cause of the accident to the failure of the flightdeck crew effectively to monitor the flight operation of the aircraft during the last four minutes before the crash. Although none of the aircraft systems were at fault, if the bulb had not failed and had not the autopilot been so easy to disengage inadvertently, the crew would not have been put in such a hazardous situation. The nose-wheel was found to be locked down.

There was a mysterious sequel to this accident which was well documented and researched in a book called *The Ghost of Flight 401*, by John G. Fuller, a science writer, which was also later made into a TV movie. Despite the force of the impact on hitting the ground in the Everglades, many parts of the major structure were still in large sections, with the equipment intact. Following the completion of the accident investigation, much of the avionics and galley equipment was salvaged, returned to the manufacturers and overhauled, to help overcome the shortages in the growing production line. The majority of this equipment was then fitted into Eastern TriStar N318EA while it was being assembled at Palmdale.

During a flight on N318EA a few months after the accident, one of the flight attendants was in the below main deck galley when she saw the apparition of Don Repo appearing in one of the ovens. She called one of her colleagues, who confirmed the vision, followed by the flight engineer, who had known Don Repo, and he communicated with him. They received a warning that there would be a fire on that particular aircraft in the future. Not long after, this TriStar had a problem develop with one of its engines at the high altitude airport of Mexico City. The TriStar was perfectly capable of a two-engine ferry flight without passengers, so approval was given. Just as the aircraft was airborne after take-off, a fire developed in one of the remaining two engines, requiring it to be shut down. With one engine operating, and the degraded performance of the hot and high airfield, with great skill, and probably some help from the supernatural, the crew managed a circuit, never going higher than 400ft (120m) above the ground, and made a safe landing.

On another occasion the same TriStar was on a turn round at Newark Airport, New York ready for a departure to Miami. It was not unusual for flight deck crews who were finished duty to return to the Miami base in a vacant first class seat. While the flightdeck crew were preparing for departure with their checks, the cabin crew were also preparing for departure including a routine head-count of the passengers. In the first class section there appeared to be an extra passenger, the unaccounted person being an Eastern Airlines' captain in uniform. When the stewardess questioned the captain's intentions, she received no response, despite repeated attempts. She was puzzled as there was no record of an Eastern Airlines' captain returning on this flight, so the aircraft captain was called from the flightdeck by which time the regular passengers in the first class cabin were becoming concerned.

Accompanied by the flight attendant, the cabin supervisor, the TriStar captain leaned over to address the mystery captain, and as he did so he froze in his tracks and said, 'My God, it's Bob Loft.' With that the mystery captain vanished and despite a thorough search, was not found, and the aircraft later departed for Miami.

There were other recorded appearances of these 'ghosts' on Eastern flights, mainly Don Repo, but the Eastern Airlines policy was to suppress the evidence, and despite a number of well documented public occurrences, any employee reporting the apparitions faced dismissal and any logbook entries were removed.

TWA N31007

The second major incident to a TriStar, fortunately without injury, was when TWA TriStar N31007 had a fire break out in the rear fuselage while it was parked locked at Boston overnight on 19 April 1974. The aircraft was a write off, although some parts were salvaged and the subsequent investigation found that the fire had started near the APU, but no reason could be determined.

Saudia HZ-AHK

A disturbing and mysterious accident happened to Saudia TriStar HZ-AHK on 19 August 1980 when carrying a total of 301 Moslem pilgrims and crew from Karachi to Mecca. The aircraft had landed at Riyadh, and soon after take-off for Jeddah, a fire was discovered in the rear cabin. The captain did not immediately turn back, but decided to return when the aircraft was about 79 miles (127km) from Riyadh although he never declared an emergency. He reported smoke in the cabin and, at 40 miles (64km) out, that there was a fire. During the approach to land, the fire melted the control cables for the throttles to the centre engine which was then shut down. On landing, still with no emergency declared, the aircraft was steered off the runway and commenced taxying, the captain requesting transport for the passengers as he planned to call an emergency evacuation. The aircraft came to a halt, but with the two wing-mounted engines still running, maintaining some residual pressurisation in the cabin which stopped the rescue services opening the doors. The engines were finally shut down six minutes after landing and it took a further five minutes to open the No 2 starboard door, by which time there was no sign of life, and the entry of further air into the cabin caused the fire to flare up and burn through the roof.

In the subsequent investigation the source of the fire appeared to be in the rearward C3 cargo hold under the cabin floor and just forward of the pressure dome, although what caused the fire was not determined due to all evidence being destroyed. The captain was criticised in the accident report for not turning back as soon as the fire was reported, not declaring an emergency and for delays after landing in taxying clear of the runway. An eye witness report also suggested that the aircraft did in fact come to a halt on the runway, and made a 180-degree turn to backtrack to the nearest exit point. The captain had asked the attending fire crew to check for any external evi-

ABOVE: The burnt-out shell of HZ-AHK at Riyadh. *Associated Press*

dence of fire, even while passengers were dying on board due to the fire and fumes in the cabin. Analysis of the cockpit voice recorder gave a sequence of events starting with the smoke detector aural warning seven minutes after take-off, but although the crew heard it they referred to the wrong check list. After three minutes the American flight engineer went into the cabin to investigate and seven minutes later a voice calls, 'Fire!', but the flight engineer reports just smoke. At this point the captain elected to turn back. At 18 minutes after the smoke warning a voice was heard to call, 'Fire in the cabin,' and the smoke was so dense that passengers were being overcome and a flight attendant could not get to the rear as the aisles were crowded with passengers. After touchdown the flight engineer suggested emergency evacuation, but the captain delayed a decision, and four minutes after touchdown, the last message from the flightdeck was, 'We are trying to evacuate now,' but no action was taken, probably because by then it was too late. When the aircraft was entered finally and the fire extinguished, bodies were found at all the exits while on the flight deck the crew were still strapped in their seats with a flight attendant laying across the central control pedestal, buried under a pile of passengers who had burst through the cockpit door. The cause of the fire was believed to be a leak of Skydrol hydraulic fluid on to some electrical cables in the rear equipment bay, which would have released toxic gas killing everyone on board before the doors could be opened.

Saudia

A less serious accident with a Saudia TriStar took place on 23 December 1980, while flying from Dharan to Karachi with 290 passengers, when the port main wheel tyres exploded during cruising at 29,000ft (8,800m). Undercarriage fragments pierced the fuselage making a 5ft by 3ft hole, the resultant decompression unfortunately sucking two children out of the aircraft. The captain made an emergency descent, and diverted to Doha, Qatar without any further incident.

Delta N726DA

A TriStar 1, N726DA of Delta, was on the approach to Dallas Fort Worth on 2 August 1985 with 163 persons on board. Just as the aircraft was approaching the runway threshold it flew through a violent thunder-storm, known as a microburst. A microburst consists of a very localised downward gust of cold air in the heart of a convective cloud. When flying into one at low altitude, the aircraft will encounter a head wind giving excess lift, followed by the violent downdraft, and then a tail-wind which reduces dramatically speed and lift, all in the space of a few seconds. The aircraft therefore becomes uncontrollable and is forced into the ground. The crew had not been warned by air traffic control about the severity of the storm, mainly because the danger had not been appreciated, and previous aircraft had landed without difficulty. When the Delta TriStar flew into the cloud it encountered airspeed fluctuations varying from plus 20kts to minus 44kts (+37 to – 81kph) from its normal approach speed, with down drafts up to 40ft (12m) per second, all within period of 32 seconds. In one second, indicated airspeed dropped from 140kts (260kph) to 120kts (180kph) and the 40ft (12m) per second downdraft changed to a 20ft (6m) per second updraft, when a strong lateral gust rolled the aircraft to the right. The angle of attack increased from six degrees to at least 23, but despite the increase in power, it could not stop the aircraft hitting the ground in a ploughed field 6,336ft (1,931m) from the threshold with the nose up and wings level. It became briefly airborne again before touching down again as it crossed a road hitting a car, killing the occupant, and starting a fire on the left side of the cabin. At this point, with the aircraft completely out of control, it began shedding parts, and it hit a water tank situated on the approach path breaking up the aircraft and destroying the forward fuselage. The aircraft was severely damaged by the impact and resulting fire, but there were 28 survivors including three cabin crew, who had been located in the mid-cabin over the wing structure, or in the relatively intact rear section. There was no evidence of any failure of the airframe, engines or equipment which could have contributed to the cause of this accident, but lessons were learned about microbursts, and many more windsheer detectors were installed at likely airports, with doppler radar being developed to help predict the problem. Unnecessary obstructions in the undershoot were also removed.

Royal Jordanian JY-AGE

A further underfuselage fire occurred on Royal Jordanian TriStar JY-AGE, on 18 October 1985 fortunately without casualties. While the aircraft was descending through 20,000ft (6,100m), there was a number 2 engine fire warning, which was shut down. This was followed by a sudden cabin decompression, filling the aircraft with smoke. The captain made an emergency landing at Singapore where it was found that an eight inch hole had been burned in the aft pressure dome also damaging two of the four hydraulic systems. The investigation concluded that the fire was probably caused by the chafing of cables from the number 2 engine generator on an adjacent air duct.

AirLanka 4R-ULD

AirLanka lost TriStar 100 4R-ULD when it was sabotaged on the ground at Colombo on 3 May 1986. Fortunately deaths were limited to 16 passengers, with injuries to a further 41, as the aircraft had been delayed on departure, and the bomb hidden in a tool box, blew the tail right off the aircraft. If it had departed on time everyone on board would have been killed, and if it had fallen in the sea, the cause would have been difficult to establish.

Delta TriStar

As a demonstration of the structural integrity and fail-safe capability of the aircraft, a Delta TriStar was on the approach to land at Newark Airport, New York on 13 November 1986 when an alert air traffic controller reported what appeared to be smoke coming from the starboard main undercarriage area. On investigation the smoke was found to be fuel vapour leaking from a fracture in the rear wing spar, and it was found that the structure had separated between the rear spar and the wing skin from the wing root to the landing gear attachment. A 6.75in (17cm) fatigue crack had reached a critical length during the latter part of the flight, this particular TriStar having flown

BELOW: The wreckage of N726DA at Grapevine, Texas. *Associated Press*

37,445 hours with 21,788 landings. A fleet-wide check of all other TriStars which had flown over 10,000 cycles showed no further sign of a similar fatigue cracking.

TWA N11002

A non-fatal, but total write off of the aircraft happened to TWA TriStar N11002 during take-off from New York, Kennedy on 30 July 1992. The aircraft was bound for San Francisco with 274 passengers and 12 crew on board when air traffic reported a fire coming from the back of the aircraft. Take-off was abandoned and the captain turned the aircraft off the runway on to soft ground, and when it came to a halt he ordered an emergency evacuation, which was carried out successfully before the aircraft was destroyed by fire.

During the subsequent investigation, it was believed that a malfunction in the stall warning system was a contributory cause to the accident. The aircraft was being flown by the first officer with two other qualified pilots and two dead-heading pilots in the cockpit. Everything appeared normal during take off to the rotation speed of 155kts (287kph). The first officer immediately felt the stall-warning stick-shaker operate and felt that the aircraft did not feel right. All the pilots on the flight deck felt that the aircraft was not performing correctly, and subsequently it was found that the starboard angle of attack indicator had been stuck at 26.1 degrees since shut down from the previous flight, and changed only with the shock of the impact, the port unit reading 12 degrees in comparison. In the accident the aircraft reached a radar altitude of 14ft (4.3m) and a climb angle of 12.6 degrees before the take-off was abandoned, touching down again at 9,400ft (2,850m) along the 14,400ft (4,400m) runway. The aircraft at a weight of 429,468lb (194,770kg) was 71,067lb (32,230kg) above the normal landing weight, the captain taking control, and applying full brakes. No doubt due to the high weight of the aircraft, the impact with the runway caused a fracture of the fuel tank structure, which is what was seen by air traffic control as fuel vapour escaping. The TriStar left the runway to one side causing the nosewheel gear to collapse, and the aircraft came to rest 30m from the centre-line, within the length of the runway. All the occupants evacuated the aircraft within about three minutes and no fire penetrated the cabin during the evacuation, but despite the efforts of the fire services, the aircraft was totally destroyed. Later inspection revealed a crack of up to 5ft (1.5m) in the starboard rear spar, no doubt caused by the over weight landing, which allowed fuel to leak from the integral wing tank. This TWA TriStar, which had flown 49,662 hours and made 19,659 landings showed no sign of fatigue in the structure.

In a 1982 edition of the *Frequent Flyer* magazine, the TriStar was quoted as being one of the cleanest, quietest and most technologically advanced aircraft ever produced. It was also one of the safest aircraft flying at the time. Flight International well known for its responsible approach to flight safety, concluded in a study of accident/incident data in January 1983 that, 'The best American widebody is the Lockheed TriStar,' and also 'the Lockheed TriStar's popular reputation as a very safe aircraft is endorsed by the record.'

BELOW: Smoke billowing from 4R-ULD's tail section. *Associated Press*

8 TriStar Production

c/n	Series	Initial Registration	Current Registration	Current Operator	Remarks
1001	1	N1011	nil	ex-Lockheed	Development, BU 8.86
1002	1	N301EA	OB-1455	Faucett	ex-Eastern, dismantled Miami 1.5.94
1003	1	N302EA	N781DL	Lockheed structural test 10.95	ex-Eastern, Delta 6.91
1004	1	N303EA	TC-RAG	AirOps	ex-Eastern, Rich Int
1005	1	N304EA	TF-ABG	Air Atlanta	ex-Eastern, wfu 16.1.84
1006	1	N305EA	N782DL	Delta	ex-Eastern
1007	1	N306EA		ex-Eastern	wfu 30.1.84 & BU 28.2.84
1008	1	D-AERY	N178AT	ATA	ex-LTU, wfu 1.95 for spares
1009	1	N308EA	N783DL	Delta 22.8.91	ex-Eastern
1010	150	N309EA	C-FTNB	Air Transat	ex-Eastern
1011	1	N310EA		ex-Eastern	wo 29.12.72 Everglades
1012	1	N311EA	N311EA	Tradewinds	ex-Eastern, wfu 22.5 85
1013	1	N31001	SE-DSE	AirOps	ex-TWA, 5 Star, ATA
1014	1	N11002			ex-TWA, Crashed JFK NY 30.7.92
1015	1	N11003		TWA	
1016	1	N11004		TWA	
1017	1	N11005		TWA	
1018	1	N11006		TWA	
1019	150	C-FTNA	C-FTNA	Air Transat	ex-Air Canada
1020	1	N313EA	N313EA	Rich International	ex-Eastern, stored 96
1021	1	C-FTNB	C-FTNB	Air Transat	ex-Air Canada, Cathay
1022	1	N314EA	TF-ABE	Air Atlanta	ex-Eastern
1023	150	C-FTNC		Air Transat	ex-Air Canada
1024	1	VR-HHV			ex-Court Line, Cathay
1025	1	A40-TP	CF-TND	Air Canada	ex-Gulf Air, Air Canada 27.10.90

BELOW: Caledonian's TriStars still operate out of Gatwick on Mediterranean routes. *Leo Marriott*

c/n	Series	Initial Registration	Current Registration	Current Operator	Remarks
1026	1	N31007			ex-TWA wo 20.4.74 Boston
1027	1	C-FTNE	VR-HOF	Cathay	ex-Air Canada, BU Avalon 5.11.94
1028	1	N31008	TWA	Stored	
1029	1	N31009	HR-AMC	AirOps	ex-TWA, bu Hurn 17.1.95
1030	1	N31010	SE-DPV	Transwede	ex-TWA, stored 96
1031	1	N31011		Marana store	ex-TWA, last op 24.10.92
1032	1	VR-HHW	TF-ABV	Air Atlanta	ex-Court Line, Cathay, ex-V2-LEM, sub-lease to Transwede as SE-DTD
1033	1	N372EA	SE-DTD	Transwede	ex-Eastern, Cathay
1034	1	N41012		L A store, spares recovery	ex-TWA, last op 24.10.92 BU 28.2.94
1035	1	N31013	TWA		
1036	1	N31014	TWA		
1037	1	N316EA	C-GTSY	Air Transat	ex-Eastern, Cathay VR-HOB, last op 11.5.96
1038	1	N317EA	N784DA	Delta 5.91	ex-Eastern
1039	1	N318EA	VR-HOI	Cathay	ex-Eastern, stored 96
1040	1	N319EA	N319EA	Rich International	ex-Eastern
1041	150	N701DA	N195AT	ATA 7.87	ex-Delta, Total Air, Air America
1042	1	N320EA	N9115G	Venada	ex-Eastern, dismantled Tucson 4.12.95
1043	1	N321EA	VR-HOD	Cathay	ex-Eastern
1044	1	N322EA	TF-ABL	Air Atlanta	ex-Eastern, Cathay
1045	1	N323EA	TF-ABP	Air Atlanta spares recovery 1.97	ex-Eastern, Cathay
1046	1	N702DA	N702TT	Total Air	ex-Delta, stored 12.93 EI-BTN
1047	1	A40-TR	CF-TNF	Air Canada, last op 26.10.90	ex-Gulf Air Marana store 11.90
1048	150	C-FTNG		Marana store	1.96 ex-Air Canada last op 27.10.90
1049	150	C-FTNH	C-FTNH	Air Transat	ex-Air Canada last op 27.10.90
1050	1	N324EA	SE-DTC	Blue Scandinavia	ex-Eastern, Cathay, Nordic East
1051	1	VR-HHY			ex-Cathay
1052	50	N703DA	N185AT	ATA 5.85	ex-Delta
1053	100	JA8501	4R-ULC	AirLanka	ex-ANA
1054	1	VR-HHX	TF-ABH	Air Atlanta	ex-Cathay
1055	1	N327EA	VR-HOK	Dragonair	ex-Eastern
1056	200	A40-TV	A40-TV	Gulf Air	stored 96
1057	50	N704DA	N192AT	ATA 3.86	ex-Delta
1058	100	C-FTNI	C-FTNI	Royal	ex-Air Canada last op 25.10.90
1059	1	N31015	SE-DSB	AirOps	ex-TWA, last op 25.10.92
1060	1	N41016	TWA		stored
1061	100	JA8502	4R-ULD	AirLanka	wo 3.5.86 Colombo
1062	100	JA8503	4R-ULE	AirLanka	ex-ANA
1063	1	N15017	TWA		
1064	100	N10112	N787M	Operation Blessing	ex-PSA, C-GIES Worldways
1065	50	N31018	SE-DSC	ex-TWA	bu Hurn by 5.9.90
1066	50	N31019	TWA		
1067	100	C-FTNJ	N140GS	Orbital Sciences	ex-Air Canada last op 28.10.90
1068	100	A40-TS	5N-BBB	ADC	ex-Gulf Air, ANA, dismantled 1.9.93

ABOVE: **Air Canada's C-FTNI.** *Leo Marriott*

BELOW: **Eastern's N319EA.** *Leo Marriott*

c/n	Series	Initial Registration	Current Registration	Current Operator	Remarks
1069	100	C-FTNK	C-FTNK	Royal	ex-Air Canada last op 27.10.90
1070	50	N762BE	N762BE	Rich International	ex-Hawaiian, ANA
1071	50	N705DA	N193AT	ATA 3.86	ex-Delta
1072	50	N41020	TF-ABM	Air Atlanta	ex-TWA last op 25.10.92, Hawaiian, SE-DPP AirOps
1073	100	C-FTNL	C-FTNL	Air Transat	ex-Air Canada last op 28.10.90
1074	50	N706DA	N186AT	ATA 4.85	ex-Delta
1075	50	N31021	OB-1545	Faucett	ex-TWA last op 13.9.92
1076	50	N31022	N196AT	ATA 3.94	ex-TWA
1077	50	N707DA	N187AT	ATA 4.85	ex-Delta
1078	50	N708DA	N188AT	ATA 10.85	ex-Delta
1079	50	N10114	N125DT	Ultimate Air Corp	ex-PSA, Worldways C-GIFE, stored 96
1080	50	N31023	TWA		
1081	50	N709DA	N189AT	ATA 9.85	ex-Delta
1082	50	N763BE	N197AT	ATA 6.91	ex-Hawaiian, ANA
1083	100	G-BBAE	G-BBAE	Caledonian	ex-BA, Worldways
1084	50	N710DA	N191AT	ATA 11.85	ex-Delta
1085	1	N329EA	D-EARC	LTU last op 6.11.92	ex-Eastern stored Mobile 12.92
1086	50	N711DA	N190AT	ATA 11.85	ex-Delta
1087	40	N330EA	OB-1504	Faucett	ex-Eastern
1088	40	N712DA	N712DA	Delta	
1089	40	N713DA	N713DA	Delta	
1090	40	N714DA	N714DA	Delta	
1091	50	N31024	TF-ABM	Air Atlanta	ex-TWA last op 25.10.92, Hawaiian
1092	40	N715DA	N715DA	Delta	

BELOW: Delta's N718DA at Los Angeles in 1993. *Leo Marriott*

c/n	Series	Initial Registration	Current Registration	Current Operator	Remarks
1093	100	G-BBAF	G-BBAF	Caledonian	ex-BA last op 5.11.90
1094	1	G-BBAG	C-GTSX	Air Transat	ex-BA last op 2.2.91, Dragonair R-HMW
1095	40	N716DA	N716DA	Delta	
1096	40	N717DA	N717DA	Delta	
1097	40	N718DA	N718DA	Delta	
1098	100	N80125		Potomac Investment	ex-TWA, last op 30.10.94, stored 96
1099	1	JA8508	C-FWCR	Air Transat	ex-ANA
1100	1	JA8509	N312GB		ex-ANA, stored
1101	100	G-BBAH	G-BBAH	Caledonian	ex-BA
1102	1	G-BBAI	G-BBAI	Caledonian	ex-BA, Worldways
1103	100	JA8510	C-GTSZ	Air Transat	ex-ANA, Total Air
1104	100	N81026		Potomac Investment	ex-TWA, last op 29.10.94, stored 96
1105	50	N765BE		Rich International	ex-Hawaiian. ANA
1106	100	G-BBAJ	G-BBAJ	Caledonian	ex-BA last op 28.10.89
1107	50	N81027		L A store	ex-TWA, last op 25.10.92, Royal spares
1108	100	N81028		Potomac Investment	ex-TWA, last op 30.10.94, stored 96
1109	100	N81029	TWA		
1110	200	HZ-AHA	HZ-AHA	Saudia	
1111	100	N31030		Potomac Investment	ex-TWA, last op 30.10.94, stored 96
1112	50	N766BE	N766BE	Rich International	ex-Hawaiian, ANA
1113	50	N764BE	N764BE	Rich International	ex-Hawaiian, ANA
1114	1	D-AERI		LTU, bu 10.91	ex-PSA, destroyed 27.6.91 Düsseldorf
1115	100	N31031	TWA		
1116	200	HZ-AHB	HZ-AHB	Saudia	

BELOW: LTU's D-AERI. *Leo Marriott*

c/n	Series	Initial Registration	Current Registration	Current Operator	Remarks
1117	1	JA8514			ex-ANA, BU 30.3.93
1118	100	VR-HHK	N155MC 10.96		ex-Cathay
1119	1	JA8515			ex-ANA, BU 30.3.93
1120	1	D-AERE	N179AT	ATA 6.95	ex-LTU, PSA stored 96
1121	40	N331EA	N785DL	Delta	stored 96 ex-Eastern, Worldways
1122	100	VR-HHL			ex-Cathay, stored 10.95
1123	40	N332EA	N786DL	Delta	ex-Eastern
1124	200	HZ-AHE	HZ-AHE	Saudia	
1125	100	D-AERU	N181AT	ATA 21.12.94	ex-LTU, PSA stored 96
1126	40	N333EA	N787DL	Delta 11.91	ex-Eastern
1127	1	JA8516	N305GB	AL Aircraft Corp	ex-ANA, last op 6.12.93
1128	1	JA8517	Air Transat		ex-ANA, dismantled 31.10.93 Marana
1129	1	JA8518	N302MB	Rich International	ex-ANA 11.93
1130	200	HZ-AHF	HZ-AHF	Saudia	
1131	200	A40-TW	200F N307GB	IAL for Arrow Air	ex-Gulf Air
1132	50	G-BEAK	200F N110GK	American International	ex-BA, last op 31.3.91 stored 96
1133	200	A40-TX	200F N308GB	IAL for Arrow Air	ex-Gulf Air
1134	1	JA8519	N300AW	Rich International	ex-ANA
1135	40	N719DA	N719DA	Delta	
1136	40	N720DA	N720DA	Delta	
1137	200	HZ-AHC	HZ-AHC	Saudia	
1138	200	A40-TY	200F N306GB	IAL for Arrow Air	ex-Gulf Air
1139	40	N721DA	N721DA	Delta	
1140	200	A40-TZ	A40-TZ	Gulf Air	stored 96
1141	40	N334EA	N788DL	Delta 9.91	ex-Eastern, stored 96
1142	40	N335EA	N789DL	Delta 9.91	ex-Eastern
1143	40	N336EA	N790DL	Delta 9.91	ex-Eastern
1144	200	HZ-AHD	HZ-AHD	Saudia	
1145	50	G-BEAL	C-CEAP	Atlanta Airways	ex-BA, & Caledonian, ex-SE-DPM
1146	50	G-BEAM	200F N112CK	American International	ex-BA last op 30.3.91 stored 96
1147	40	N722DA	N722DA	Delta	
1148	200	HZ-AHG	HZ-AHG	Saudia	
1149	200	HZ-AHH	HZ-AHH	Saudia	
1150	40	N723DA	N723DA	Delta	
1151	200	N724DA	N724DA	Delta	
1152	1	D-AERP	N	Avtec for freighter mods	ex-LTU, Eastern, stored due to overweight.
1153	1	D-AERM	N183AT	ATA 28.5.95	ex-LTU, Eastern
1154	1	JA8520		Air Transat	ex-ANA, dismantled 31.1.94 Marana
1155	1	JA8521	N310GB	Rich International	ex-ANA, stored
1156	1	JA8522	N309GB	Rich International	ex-ANA
1157	500	G-BFCA	KC.1 ZD948	216 Sq	ex-BA
1158	200	D-AERN	200F N851MA	ILFC for Millon Air	ex-LTU, Eastern
1159	500	G-BFCB	K.1 ZD949	216 Sq	ex-BA
1160	200	HZ-AHI	HZ-AHI	Saudia	

c/n	Series	Initial Registration	Current Registration	Current Operator	Remarks
1161	200	HZ-AHJ	HZ-AHJ	Saudia	
1162	40	N725DA	N725DA	Delta	
1163	1	N726DA	N726DA	Delta	Crashed Dallas 1.8.85
1164	500	G-BFCC	KC1 ZD950	216 Sq	ex-BA
1165	500	G-BFCD	K1 ZD951	216 Sq	ex-BA
1166	500	N751DA	N751DA	Delta	
1167	40	N727DA	N727DA	Delta	
1168	500	G-BFCE	KC1 ZD952	216 Sq	ex-BA
1169	200	HZ-AHK		Saudia	wo 14.8.80 Riyadh
1170	200	HZ-AHL	HZ-AHL	Saudia	
1171	200	HZ-AHM	HZ-AHM	Saudia	
1172	500	N752DA	N752DA	Delta	
1173	40	N728DA	N728DA	Delta	
1174	500	G-BFCF	KC1 ZD953	216 Sq	ex-BA
1175	200	HZ-AHN	HZ-AHN	Saudia	
1176	500	N501PA	N759DA	Delta	ex-PanAm, United
1177	500	N503PA	C2 ZE706	216 Sq	ex-PanAm
1178	200	G-BGBB	200F N105CK	American International	ex-BA, ex-Air Lanka 4R-ULN, stored 96

BELOW: **ZD950, a KC1 of No 216 Squadron.** *Marshall Aerospace*

1179	500	9Y-TGJ	9Y-TGJ	BWIA	
1180	40	N729DA	N729DA	Delta	
1181	500	N504PA	N754DL	Delta	ex-PanAm
1182	200	G-BGBC	200F N107CK	American International	ex-BA last op 31.10.91 stored 96
1183	500	D-AERT	D-AERT	LTU	stored
1184	500	N505PA	N755DL	Delta	ex-PanAm
1185	500	N507PA	N756DR	Delta	ex-PanAm
1186	500	N508PA	C.2A ZE704	216 Sq	ex-PanAm
1187	200	HZ-AHO	HZ-AHO	Saudia	
1188	500	N509PA	C.2A ZE705	216 Sq	ex-PanAm
1189	500	N753DA	N753DA	Delta	
1190	200	HZ-AHP	HZ-AHP	Saudia	
1191	500	9Y-TGN	9Y-TGN	BWIA	
1192	200	HZ-AHQ	HZ-AHQ	Saudia	
1193	200	G-BHBL	200F N104CK	American International	ex-BA last op 27.10.91
1194	500	N510PA	N760DH	Delta	ex-PanAm, United
1195	500	N511PA	VR-CGF	Jet Stream Holding	ex-PanAm, United, LTU, last op 1.2.94, stored
1196	500	D-AERL	JY-AGF	Alia	ex-LTU, last op 30.4.96
1197	500	N512PA	N763DL	Delta 5.89	ex-PanAm, United
1198	200	G-BHBM	200F N102CK	American International	ex-BA last op 6.11.91
1199	40	N730DA	N730DA	Delta	
1200	40	N1731D	N1731D	Delta	
1201	200	N92TA	A40-TA	Gulf	stored 96, returned to service 97
1202	500	C-GAGF	N764DA	Delta 8.91	ex-Air Canada
1203	200	N92TB	A40-TB	Gulf	stored 96, returned to service 97
1204	200	G-BHBN		American International	ex-BA, last op 7.5.91 stored Mojave 96
1205	200	G-BHBO		American International	ex-BA, last op 21.3.91 stored Mojave 96
1206	500	C-GAGG	N765DA	Delta 8.91	ex-Air Canada
1207	500	C-GAGH	N766DA	Delta	ex-Air Canada 1.92
1208	500	N513PA	N761DA	Delta	ex-PanAm, United
1209	500	C-GAGI	N767DA	Delta	ex-Air Canada last op 27.10.91
1210	500	N514PA	N762DA	Delta	ex-PanAm, United
1211	200	G-BHBP	200F N106CK	American International	ex-BA, AirLanka lease
1212	200	G-BHBR	200F N103CK	American International	ex-BA last op 8.11.91
1213	40	N1732D	N1732D	Delta	
1214	200	HZ-AHR	HZ-AHR	Saudia	
1215	100	N31032	SE-DSD	AirOps, stored 96	ex-TWA last op 25.10.92
1216	500	C-GAGJ	N768DL	Delta	ex-Air Canada last op 28.10.91
1217	500	JY-AGA	JY-AGA	Alia	
1218	500	C-GAGK	N769DL	Delta	ex-Air Canada 1.92
1219	500	JY-AGB	JY-AGB	Alia	
1220	500	JY-AGC	JY-AGC	Alia	
1221	100	N31033	C-GRYU	Royal	ex-TWA last op 24.10.92, Air Atlanta
1222	500	9Y-THA	9Y-THA	BWIA	
1223	200	A40-TT	A40-TT	Gulf	stored, returned to service 97
1224	40	N733DS	N733DS	Delta	
1225	40	N1734D	N1734D	Delta	

1226	40	N735D	N735D	Delta	
1227	250	N736DY	N736DY	Delta	
1228	250	N737D	N737D	Delta	
1229	500	JY-AGD	JY-AGD	Alia	
1230	100	N8034T	N194AT	ATA	ex-TWA last op 25.10.92
1231	100	N7035T	SE-DPR	Time Air	ex-TWA last op 25.10.92
1232	100	N7036T		TWA	
1233	500	N3140D	9Y-THB	BWIA	
1234	250	N1738D	N1738D	Delta	
1235	500	4R-ULA	Air Lanca	G-BLUS with BA	
1236	500	4R-ULB	Air Lanca	G-BLUT with BA	
1237	250	N1739D	N1739D	Delta	
1238	500	JY-AGE	JY-AGE	Alia	
1239	500	CS-TEA	CS-TEA	TAP	leased to LAM
1240	500	CS-TEB	ex-V2-LEO	TAP	ex-Air Mauritius lease
1241	500	CS-TEC	CS-TEC	TAP	leased to TAAG
1242	500	CS-TED	CS-TED	TAP	to Air Transat 2.97
1243	500	CS-TEE	CS-TEE	TAP	to Air Transat 1.97
1244	250	N740DA	N740DA	Delta	
1245	250	N741DA	N741DA	Delta	
1246	500	JY-AGI	V2-LEJ	Caribjet, leased to Air India	ex-Alia, TAP
1247	500	JY-HKJ	JY-HKJ	Jordanian Royal Flight	
1248	500	JY-AGJ	V2-LEK	Caribjet, leased to Air India	ex-Alia, TAP
1249	500	JY-AGH	HZ-HM6	Govt of Saudi Arabia	ex-JY-AGH Alia
1250	500	7T-VRA	HZ-HM5	Govt of Saudi Arabia	Algerian VIP Flt, not delivered

BELOW: **Royal Jordanian JY-AGC.** *Leo Marriott*

9 CHRONOLOGY

29 March 1968
TriStar programme launched by combined initial order from Eastern and TWA.

13 August 1968
Initial run of RB211 engine at Derby.

1 March 1969
Fabrication of the first TriStar commenced.

24 June 1969
Assembly of the first aircraft commenced.

6 March 1970
First flight of RB211 engine in VC-10 testbed.

27 April 1970
First wing delivered to Palmdale by Avco.

20 July 1970
Ronald Reagan dedicates the new Palmdale facility.

1 September 1970
Roll-out of first TriStar.
PSA announce order for two TriStars.

16 November 1970
Maiden flight of prototype TriStar from Palmdale.

4 February 1971
Financial collapse of Rolls-Royce.

15 February 1971
Second TriStar joins test programme.

23 February 1971
Rolls-Royce nationalised.

27 April 1971
First automatic landing.

17 May 1971
Third TriStar makes first flight.

9 September 1971
US Government approved loan guarantees, keeping Lockheed in business, and allowing the TriStar programme to continue.

24 October 1971
Fourth TriStar first flight.

2 December 1971
Fifth, and final development TriStar flew.

27 December 1971
Provisional FAA certification granted.

BELOW: TWA received L-1011-1 N81028 in July 1975. Converted to a -100 in March 1978, to a -200 in April 1978 and a -500 in May 1980, N81028 was still going strong in September 1990 when this photograph was taken. *Leo Marriott*